FOUR ESSAYS
ON THE
SHAKESPEARE AUTHORSHIP
QUESTION

This book was designed and edited by Jerri-Jo Idarius of Creation-Designs which is based in Willits, California, USA. It was printed by CreateSpace, a DBA of On-Demand Publishing LLC, part of the Amazon group of companies.

For additional copies or to correspond with the author, contact him by email at: michaeladair69@yahoo.com

The cover image is of Edward de Vere and was painted by Cornelus Ketel circa 1580. It is known as the Ashbourne Portrait. This version of the Ashbourne is a reproduction of the painting as it existed from its discovery in 1847 through a series of cleanings which occurred up to the year 1979, when it underwent two periods of major restoration work under the direction of the Folger Shakespeare Library. Reproduction of this painting is used by permission of the Folger Shakespeare Library.

Publishing history
First edition, January 2011
Second edition (revised), September 2011

ISBN-13: 978-0615527932

FOUR ESSAYS
ON THE
SHAKESPEARE AUTHORSHIP
QUESTION

MIKE A'DAIR

Verisimilitude Press, Willits, California

Contents

INTRODUCTION

These four essays are offered as an introduction to the Shakespeare Authorship Question. They are a distillation of the many works that I have read since 2003, and are intended for the general reader.

In the first essay I give fifty-five reasons why William Shakspere, the man from Stratford, cannot have been the true author of the Works of William Shakespeare. The second essay offers forty-eight reasons why Edward de Vere, the Seventeenth Earl of Oxford, was Shakespeare. The third essay explores the secret identity of Edward de Vere, i.e., why even his recently excavated biography as the shining but shrouded Seventeenth Earl of Oxford does not fully explain who he was. The fourth essay is a brief biography of Shakespeare based on the knowledge that many scholars and researcheers have uncovered since 1920.

Throughout the book I've included footnoted references because I want the reader to understand that I am not making this stuff up. It is all documented and, although my conclusions may be questioned, I would assert that they are defensible and that they explain de Vere more fully and more reasonably than other, more pedestrian, claims and assumptions about his life.

Mike A'Dair
Willits, California
August 18, 2010

FIFTY-FIVE QUESTIONS ABOUT WILLIAM SHAKESPEARE

William Shakespeare is the greatest poet and dramatist in the English language. Most people accept his standard biography, which runs roughly as follows.

William Shakespeare was born in Stratford upon Avon, England, in April, 1564, the son of an illiterate glover and wool merchant who served honorably in the local government for many years before being crushed by debt. He may have gone to the King's New School in Stratford, but there is no record of it, nor is there any record of his having attended any college or university in England or elsewhere.

On November 27, 1582, an entry was made in the official records of Worcester for a bond for a marriage license between "William Shaxpere and Anne Whately of Temple Grafton," a small village some five miles west of Stratford. (1)

However, that marriage did not take place, as on the next day, November 28, 1582, a marriage license was granted to "William Shagspere and Anne Hathwey." Hathaway, as she is now known, was eight years older than Shakespeare and was three months pregnant at the time of their marriage.

She gave birth to Susanna Shakespeare in May, 1583, and to twins, Judith and Hamnet, in 1585. It is generally supposed that Shakespeare left Hathaway soon after the birth of the twins to seek his fortune on the stage. However, the couple remained married.

For the next seven years, his activities and whereabouts are unknown. In 1592, a reference was made in a pamphlet written by London author and playwright Robert Greene to an "upstart crow beautified with our feathers"… who "is in his own conceit the only Shake-scene in a country." Most scholars have accepted that the referent is William Shakespeare and, based upon the reference, assume that he had embarked upon his career as a playwright and actor a year or two prior to that date.

In 1593, while London theatres were closed by the plague, Shakespeare published the long narrative poem *Venus and Adonis*. The following year he published another long narrative poem, *The Rape of Lucrece*. In that year also The Lord

Chamberlain's Men, England's premier theatre troupe, was formed, with Shakespeare playing an integral part as actor, playwright and paymaster. He also became a shareholder in the Globe Theatre by 1599.

His plays began to see publication, at first anonymously beginning in 1594, and then under his own name beginning in 1598. In 1596, his father was granted a long-sought and previously denied family coat of arms. In August of the same year, his son Hamnet died at age 11. The next year, William Shakespeare bought New Place, the second best house in Stratford upon Avon.

From 1596 to 1604, while writing such classics as *Hamlet* and *Julius Caesar*, Shakespeare lived in various districts in and around London. He did not buy a house there but rather moved from place to place about every two years. During these years he was sought several times, apparently unsuccessfully, by legal authorities for failure to pay his taxes.

The Elizabethan equivalent of a restraining order was placed against him in 1596 in order to protect a William Wayte of London. The bond which pleads for sureties of the peace to protect Wayte states that "William Shakspare," Dorothy Soer, Ann Lee and Francis Langley are to keep away from Wayte, who feared "death and mutilation of his limbs" at the hands of the four. Langely was the owner of the then newly built Swan Theatre. (2)

He was also involved in several lawsuits in Stratford at this time, and in February 1598 was listed among those in Stratford who hoarded corn or malt during a local food shortage. From about 1602 to 1604, he lived in a rented room in the home of the Mountjoys, a French Hugoenot family who lived in the Cripplegate section of London.

After 1604, available records suggest that he removed permanently back to Stratford, where, in addition to writing *King Lear, Antony and Cleopatra, The Winter's Tale* and *The Tempest*, he continued to engage in various business and real estate ventures and in litigation. (3) His book *Shake-speares Sonnets* was published in 1609, but seems to have been quickly suppressed.

In January 1616, he wrote his will, in which he left his wife his second best bed. He died in April 1616, apparently on his birthday, and is buried in the Holy Trinity Church in Stratford.

For many people who have studied this biography it is becoming increasingly difficult to believe that this man, who alternately seems to have spelled his last name Shakspere, Shagrxsxe or Spbtsps—four of his extant six signatures can in good faith only be described as illegible scrawls—was the author of the Works of William Shakespeare. The following are a few of the many questions that arise when one attributes the authorship of the Works to the Stratford man.

Note: When the author of the plays is being referred to, the last name is spelled

Shakespeare. When the Stratford man is being referred to, the last name is spelled the way he spelled it: Shakspere.

1. Why are his six extant signatures so poorly written?

2. Why do we have no letters by him?

3. Why did he not teach his daughters to read?

4. Why do neither Oxford University nor Cambridge University have any records of his having gone to college there?

5. Why are none of his plays set in Stratford?

6. Why are there no characters in his plays who speak with a Warwickshire dialect?

7. Why were his books or his manuscripts not mentioned in his will?

8. Why are his plays always written from the point of view of the aristocracy? All his heroes are either royal or from the nobility and the common people—people from his own class—are always portrayed in an unflattering light.

9. Why, if he was a member of the lower classes—the son of an impoverished glover—are none of his 37 plays about the common man making good?

10. Several of the plays display a first hand knowledge of the geography, people and customs of Italy and France. How could a commoner whose possessions in London, according to London tax assessment records, were valued at five pounds in 1596, have been able to afford a trip to Italy and France?

11. A careful examination of Shakespeare's sources indicates that he stopped reading and going to the theatre after 1603. (4) Also scholars have pointed out that, with the exception of *The Tempest*, there is no contemporary social or political reference in the plays that is later than 1604. (5) Yet he is thought to have continued writing until 1611 or 1612. Why would Shakespeare have ceased to gather new knowledge and material in 1603, ostensibly his 39th year?

12. With regard to *The Tempest*, contemporary researchers Lynn Kositsky and Roger Stritmatter have determined that the alleged source material for *The Tempest*, (*True Reportary* by William Strachey) was likely written in 1610 and was probably in England not earlier than 1612. It was not published until 1625. (6)

So how could William Shakspere, who was living in Stratford in 1611, have gotten hold of the manuscript and incorporated it into *The Tempest*, which orthodox scholars believe was first produced in that year?

13. From November 1604 to February 1605, the recently crowned King James held the world's first Shakespeare festival. Of the ten plays that were produced in that holiday court theatre season, eight were by Shakespeare and two were by Ben Jonson. What was so special about the year 1604, that no play by the author contained material from after that year, and that in that year was held the first celebration of the author's works?

14. In October 1615, Thomasina Heminges Ostler filed suit against her father, the actor John Heminges, seeking to gain legal recognition of a portion of the investors' shares of the Globe Theatre, which she believed was due her through the death of her husband, actor and Globe Theatre shareholder William Ostler. In her lawsuit, which was written in Latin, Mrs. Ostler wrote, … "ad firmam tradisisset quibusdam Cuthberto Burbadge and Ricardo Burbadge de Londonia generosis, prefato Willelmo Shakespeare and Augustino Phillips and Thome Pope de Londonia generosis defunctis…" Translated into English, the Latin means, " to Richard and Cuthbert Burbage, gentlemen of London, and to William Shakespeare, Augustine Phillips and Thomas Pope of London, dead gentlemen." (7)

In other words, Thomasina Ostler, widow of dead actor William Ostler and presumably knowledgable about the inner workings of the King's Men and the Globe Theatre, claimed in her lawsuit that William Shakespeare was a "dead gentleman" in 1615. Yet William Shakspere of Stratford died in April of 1616. Was Mrs. Ostler misinformed, or are we?

15. Reverend John Ward was vicar of Stratford upon Avon from 1662 to 1681. During those years he kept a diary, which has become an important bulwark in authenticating the life of Shakespeare as the author of the Works. However, Ward's diaries are a double edged sword; they raise more questions about Shakespeare than they answer.

There are sixteen diaries in all. Of those sixteen volumes, Ward only mentions Shakespeare in the first volume. He notes that Shakespeare had two daughters, that one had married a local physician, and that he, Shakespeare, was thought locally to be a "natural wit, without any art at all." Ward goes on to jot down a rumor he had heard that Shakespeare "spent at the rate of a thousand pounds a year."

That is all Ward writes about Shakespeare, in sixteen diaries spanning a nineteen year period during his life as vicar of Stratford.

Is it credible that a man who was interested in Shakespeare and who was living in the Bard's home town just half a century after his death would have heard nothing noteworthy about that town's most illustrious son over a nineteen year period? Why did the Stratford folk not have more stories about the man whose life was memorialized on the chancel wall of its Holy Trinity Church? Or, if they did have more stories, why did Ward not write them down?

16. The death of William Shakespeare in April 1616 was unremarked by both the public and by other authors. This is in contradistinction to what occurred after the deaths of other notable contemporary literary and theatrical figures.

   For example, after Edmund Spenser's death in 1599, his coffin was carried by a host of poets to Westminster Abbey and he was laid to rest amid great ceremony near the tomb of Chaucer. Noted poets read laudatory poems to his memory. Francis Beaumont's death in 1616 merited a similar show of respect. Actor Richard Burbage's death in 1619 brought a cloud of gloom over all London and five epitaphs to his memory were published. Francis Bacon's death in 1626 was honored by the publication of thirty-two Latin elegies. Poet Michael Drayton, now remembered chiefly for his little-read collection of sonnets, *Idea*, was honored by a funeral procession to Westminster Abbey. The next year a monument to Drayton was erected in the abbey, as well. Ben Jonson's death in 1636 "was mourned within six months by a whole book of verses by the leading poets of the day." (8)

   Yet the death of William Shakespeare occasioned none of this. Why?

17. William Shakespeare was unmentioned by several contemporary surveys of the literature of the period. True, he was mentioned, famously, by Francis Meres in *Palladis Tamia* (1598.) But in other reviews in which he seemingly should have been mentioned, he was not. These include *Skialetheia* (1598), T*he New Metamorphosis* (1600 to 1615) *Abuses Stript and Whipt* (1613) and Henry Peacham's *The Complete Gentleman* (1622).

   We know his work was highly regarded by his contemporaries. Numerous editions of his plays were published in pirated editions. The long poems, *Venus and Adonis* and *The Rape of Lucrece*, were repeatedly published in numerous editions between 1593 and 1630. In the winter of 1604-1605, eight of his plays were performed in the court of King James I, essentially constituting the world's first Shakespeare festival.

   Yet, in spite of these successes, William Shakespeare was passed over in at least four contemporary critical essays on the literature of the period. Why?

18. William Camden was a notable man of the period. He was Clarencieux

King of Arms, and as such was responsible for granting John Shakspere a coat of arms in 1596. He was the headmaster of Westminster School, and as such was Ben Jonson's teacher. He was also the first historian of the reign of Queen Elizabeth, for which he was given access to the governmental and private documents from William Cecil, Lord Burghley.

Camden is guilty of a strange omission concerning William Shakespeare. In 1605, in his book *Remains*, Camden named Shakespeare as being one of the "most pregnant wits of our times, whom succeeding ages may justly admire." Yet in his *Britannia* (1607), when discussing the most illustrious people to have come from Stratford upon Avon, he does not mention William Shakespeare. (9) Why?

19. William Shakespeare seems to have had a schizophrenic attitude toward his writings. On the one hand, we know from the sonnets that he was certain his work would live forever. For he says in Sonnet 55:

> Not marble, nor the gilded monuments
> Of princes, shall outlive this pow'rful rhyme…

And in Sonnet 18 , the poet asserts that his art will defeat Death.

> But thy eternal summer shall not fade,
> Nor lose possession of that fair thou ow'st,
> Nor shall Death brag thou wand'rest in his shade,
> When in eternal lines to time thou grow'st.

Of course, his plays have drawn the highest praise from critics, philosophers, actors and directors, from other poets and creative writers, from artists, from lovers and from people who wish they were lovers. Except for the dark period of the English Civil War, they have never been absent from the stage, from about 1588 or so, (the earliest reference to *Hamlet* was published in 1589) until the present day.

So, somehow, Shakespeare was right. His words have become immortal and, as far as anything human can be said to have become eternal, his writings have assumed the mantle of eternity.

But at the same time, the history of publication of the plays and poems has a number of anomalies which, given Shakespeare's attitude toward his writings, seem inexplicable. For example, the first four of his plays to have been published, *Titus Andronicus*, *2 Henry VI* and *3 Henry VI*, and *Romeo and Juliet*, were published anonymously. Why did Shakespeare, who believed his works would live forever, not care if his plays were published with his name on them?

20. According to Diana Price, 15 of the 33 individual editions of the plays that were published before the First Folio in 1623, were published with the author's name spelled as "Shake-speare," that is, with a hyphen. (10) This is important, because it implies either that Shakespeare did not know how to spell his name, or he didn't care, or that he regarded it, about half the time, as a pseudonym. Why was the author's name printed as Shake-speare in 45 percent of the plays published before 1623, and in the title of *Shake-speare's Sonnets* and as the author of *A Lover's Complaint*?

21. Many of the plays, prior to publication in the First Folio, including *Hamlet*, *King Lear* and *Romeo and Juliet*, were published in notoriously poor quarto editions. The First Folio itself is rife with errors. Here is author Charlton Ogburn, Jr., commenting on the quality of the First Folio.

"The sheets of the Folio as they were first pulled from Jaggard's presses abounded in errors, which were corrected as the printing proceeded so that probably no two copies of the more than one thousand printed were alike. What remained, however, was an edition in which in some places the names of actors are printed instead of those of characters, poetry is sometimes rendered as prose, and luminous passages in the quartos are passed over. According to A. W. Pollard, 'the Folio prints abut three times as many errors in *Richard II* as in the quarto.'... In other words, far from giving us the plays of Shakespeare "perfect in their limbs" and "absolute in their numbers, as he conceived them," the Folio in numerous instances does not even come up to the earlier quartos." (11) So why did William Shakespeare regard the greatest works in the history of the English language, works which he himself thought would live forever, as not worth correcting and, apparently, not worth preserving?

22. Assuming that, from the close of his writing career about 1612 until his death in 1616, he had sufficient time for the task, and accepting that he wanted his writings to live forever and that he thought they would live forever, and assuming that he had the financial means to do so, why did Shakespeare not bring out an edition of his writings during his life?

23. Let us reflect on the education that the author had. He had a very thorough and detailed familiarity with classical Greek and Latin literature, drama and poetry, as well as with French, Italian, and Spanish languages and literature. He was well versed in the law, medicine, natural history, flora and fauna of England, English history, Roman, Greek and European history, the Bible, military arts, naval terminology, as well as the sports and pastimes of the upper classes, such as falconry, archery, chivalrous tournaments, sword fighting and fencing. The author was superbly educated and informed, one of the best educated men in the world at that time, and

at any time. So how could the Stratford man, who according to tradition left the King's New School in Stratford at age thirteen and who did not attend either Oxford or Cambridge or any school in England or in Europe that we know of, have attained such a superb education?

24. Some of the plays appear to have sources which, while they seem to have been available to William Shakespeare, could not have been available to William Shakspere. For example, *Two Gentlemen of Verona*, which is thought to have been written in 1594 and to be one of the author's earliest plays, contains elements of commedia dell' arte, commedia erudita, Greek romance and continental European Renaissance pastoral traditions. Literature that has been identified as source material for *Two Gentlemen*, including Greek romance and the continental pastoral novels, was not available in English until 1596, too late to have influenced that play. (12) So why does the play follow so closely these stories and poems? How could Shakespeare have drawn upon source material that he could not have read?

25. Assuming that the reason that Shakespeare knew the source materials for *Two Gentlemen of Verona* is because he read them in the original, how did he come to learn Spanish and Italian?

26. The commedia dell'arte question is also problematical. One scholar, Allardyce Nicol, writing in 1963, has found commedia dell'arte influence in ten Shakespeare plays. (13) But commedia dell'arte theatre was not being performed in England in the early 1590s, when the commedia-influenced plays, such as *Two Gentlemen of Verona* and *A Comedy of Errors*, are thought to have been written. A few commedia troupes did come to England in the 1570s, but they did not perform widely throughout the land and it is doubtful that the Stratford lad would have seen an Italian troupe performing commedia dell'arte in Stratford. (14) So how could Shakespeare have assimilated a commedia dell'arte influence, as he clearly did?

27. The dedications to the two long poems, *Venus and Adonis* but especially *The Rape of Lucrece*, are problematical. The dedication to *Lucrece* reads, "The love I dedicate to your Lordship is without end; whereof this pamphlet without beginning is but a superfluous moiety. The warrant I have of your honorable disposition, not the worth of my untutored lines, makes it assured of acceptance. What I have done is yours, what I have to do is yours, being part in all I have, devoted yours. Were my worth greater, my duty would show greater; meantime, as it is, it is bound to your Lordship, to whom I wish long life still lengthened with all happiness."

It is a remarkable dedication, the more so because it is inscribed to Henry Wriothesley, the Third Earl of Southampton. Therefore, the phrase "being part in all I have, devoted yours" implies that the author had devoted all his life, his soul, to the Earl of Southampton. It is virtually a marriage vow; moreover, it is a marriage vow publicly proclaimed by an actor to a high ranking nobleman. In those days, this was not done; it bordered on a criminal act.

The uniqueness of the *Lucrece* dedication has not gone unnoticed by scholars. Professor D. Nichol Smith says of it, "There is no other dedication like this in Elizabethan literature." (15) Even Stratfordian biographer Stephen Greenblatt calls it "not at all typical." (16) Why would and how could a commoner publicly proclaim that degree of love to a nobleman?

28. Three biographers of Henry Wriothesley, Third Earl of Southampton, have labored unsuccessfully to corroborate the presumed connection between the earl and William Shakespeare. These were Charlotte Stopes, author of *The Life of Henry, Third Earl of Southampton* (1922), G. P. V. Akrigg, author of *Shakespeare and the Earl of Southampton* (1968) and Alfred Rowse, who wrote *Shakespeare's Southampton* (1965.)

According to writers Dorothy and Charlton Ogburn, Senior, Charlotte Stopes spent eight years looking through public and private records searching for corroboration that Shakespeare and Southampton knew each other; she failed to find any evidence. (17) "A later biographer, G. P. V. Akrigg, gained access to newly discovered Southampton family archives, but he didn't find anything, either." (18) "We have no evidence as to when, where or under what circumstances William Shakespeare first met the Earl of Southampton," Akrigg wrote. (19)

According to Charlton Ogburn, Jr., their fate was shared by the third biographer, Rowse. (20)

So we have two of the most passionate and iconoclastic of dedications in English literature, written by a low-born, provincially raised actor to a young nobleman, and beyond those dedications, we have no proof that the two men knew each other. How could that be?

29. The chronology of the composition of the plays seems counter-intuitive. If we accept the Stratfordian paradigm, we have seven plays—*Timon of Athens, Coriolanus, Pericles, Cymbeline, The Winter's Tale, The Tempest* and *Henry VIII*, that are regarded as having been written in a long denouement period, after the composition of the great tragedies. When compared with the tragedies, the quality of these plays is problematical. With some of them, it is as if the author must have forgotten how to write, the difference is so great. How can this falling off be explained?

30. The book *Shake-speares Sonnets*, which appears to be the chronicle of the author's love affair with a much younger man, was published in 1609, during

the putative author's lifetime. Most orthodox critics and scholars agree that the sonnets were likely written in the early 1590s, when the putative author would have been less than 30 years old. Yet, a number of the sonnets describe a man who is in his middle years, or older than his middle years, who is "beated and chopped with a tanned antiquity" (Sonnet 62); whose days are "past the best" (Sonnet 138); who has been "made lame by fortune's dearest spite" (Sonnet 37); who reflects on his life, "my grief lies onward and my joy behind" (Sonnet 50); who warns the Fair Youth that a time is coming, "when forty winters shall besiege thy brow" (Sonnet 2) and who repeatedly admonishes him to father a child. How could and why would a 28 year old write so relentlessly about the griefs of middle age?

31. Some scholars, such as Margaret Chute (*Shakespeare of London*, 1949) maintain that by the early Jacobean period, when William Shakespeare was supposed to have written his greatest tragedies, other playwrights had developed beyond him stylistically and that, "it was only the old-fashioned dramatists like William Shakespeare who still wrote the kind of play that had once been popular with everyone." How is it possible that the greatest poet of the English language would be an anachronism while he was still writing, and that he would be superceded in sophistication by those to whom he is supposed to be incomparably superior?

32. Again, chronology. If the sonnets were written in the early 1590s and the plays written 1588 to 1611, then the early light-hearted comedies—*The Comedy of Errors, Two Gentlemen of Verona, The Taming of the Shrew, Love's Labour's Lost*—were written at the same time that those dark, grieving sonnets of middle age, which were ostensibly written by a poet who was less than 30 years old.

Also, those same light-hearted comedies were written when the Queen was approaching or past 60, and when there was no clear successor to the throne. It was a dark brooding period of diminishing Elizabethan charisma, filled with war and the rumors of war, when the heroes and values of the mid-Elizabethan period were dead or dying. It was a period of uncertainty and waiting. The mood of the early plays, which were allegedly written between 1588 to 1594 or so, don't match the contemporary mood of the kingdom nor of the sonnets. Why?

33. In the sonnets, once again we have clear indications that the author was a nobleman. In Sonnet 91, for example, the poet writes "Some glory in their birth" – which would be allowed for a middle or lower class poet to write, assuming that he was a keen observer of the life around him. But in the same poem he writes, "Thy love is better than high birth to me," which implies that the poet was himself nobly born.

In Sonnet 69, Shakespeare criticizes the Fair Youth, admonishing him that, "thou dost common grow." The implication is that, to the author, being common, or not of noble birth, is a shameful condition. Why would William Shakespeare, ostensibly the son of an illiterate glover and wool merchant, write as if he were a man of high birth?

34. Sonnet 10 offers another mind-bending conundrum, for in it the poet tells the Fair Youth, "Make thee another self for love of me." The line comes in the midst of the first seventeen sonnets, which largely plead with an unknown "Fair Youth" to marry and beget children in order to propagate his house and himself. If we accept that the poet is the Stratford man, an actor, poet and playwright who springs from common stock, and if we accept that the Fair Youth of the poem is aristocratic (for why else would the poet admonish him that he does "common grow"?) then we run into even more trouble trying to make sense of a common-born poet pleading with an aristocratic youth to father a child "for love of me." What possible relationship could a middle or lower class poet—an actor, no less—have with a nobly born youth which would justify his asking the youth to father a child "for love of me"?

35. To continue with the sonnets, once we accept that the poet had a relationship with the Fair Youth which would entitle him to claim the prerogatives associated with the closest of human ties, then why would the Poet proceed to, in subsequent poems, address the Fair Youth in terms of idealized adulation and homosexual passion? Assuming that the dedication to the sonnets was written by someone who had an understanding of the conditions under which the poems were written, and that therefore the sonnets had one single person who begat or inspired them, then how could the Poet move from being a sort of spiritual coach of the Wayward Youth, urging him to beget children and thereby preserve both his beauty and his house, to becoming the youth's lover? What the hell is going on in these poems?

36. Many scholars believe that the sonnets are mere exercises and that they had nothing to do with, and can shed no light upon, Shakespeare's actual life. This view has been held for centuries. The late 18th Century critic George Steevens castigated his younger contemporary Edmund Malone when Malone ventured into the murky waters of attempting to deduce a biography of the poet from the sonnets.

In the mid-19th Century, Bolton Corney wrote that the sonnets "are, with very slight exceptions, mere poetical exercises." (21) Two of Shakespeare's most highly respected establishment biographers, Sir Sidney Lee and Joseph Quincy Adams, also dismissed the biographical aspect of the sonnets. Lee said it was of "slender proportions" and Adams wrote that, in the sonnets, Shakespeare was participating in a "trial of skill with his fellow poets." (22) Another Shakespearean biographer, Marchette Chute, almost warned the reader not to think about whether the sonnets came from Shakespeare's life or his imagination. "Very little can actually be said about the sonnets," she wrote. "No single theory can be safely formed about them." (23)

Is it possible that these poems are, as Corney opined, "mere poetical exercises"? How could it be possible that the poet would obsessively, relentlessly, almost pathologically, in poem after poem, great, mediocre and poor, return to the same theme, if he stood under no emotional compulsion to do so?

37. But if they are not "mere poetical exercises", then how can we deduce any kind of a reasonable authorial life from the sonnets? How can we square the lame, poor, despised, guilty, licentious, bisexual nobleman whose ghostly image rises from the lines of the sonnets with the putative author, the ruthless businessman and elusive universal genius from Stratford?

38. The dedication to the sonnets is, if possible, even more mysterious than the two dedications to the long narrative poems. Here it is:

TO.THE.ONLIE.BEGETTER.OF.
THESE.INSUING.SONNETS.
M^r. W. H. ALL.HAPPINESSE.
AND.THAT.ETERNITIE.
PROMISED.
BY.

OUR.EVER-LIVING.POET.
WISHETH.

THE.WELL-WISHING.
ADVENTURER.IN.
SETTING.
FORTH.

T.T.

What does the phrase, "wisheth the well-wishing adventurer in setting forth" mean? It is a bizarre usage, yet not clumsy or hackneyed or unlettered. Why does the author use the words "wisheth" and "well-wishing" so closely together, in the same sentence, saying the same thing?

39. Who wrote the dedication, William Shakespeare or the publisher, Thomas Thorpe?

40. Why does the dedication have a period after each word? Do those periods mean anything? If they do mean something, what could they mean?

41. Does the dedication say that Mr. W.H. is the only begetter of these ensuing sonnets? Can that mean that someone whose initials were W.H. was the inspiration of the sonnets?

42. Who was Mr. W.H.?

43. The memorial bust of William Shakespeare, which is carved into the chancel wall of the Holy Trinity Church in Stratford upon Avon, presents a host of problems, chief of which is that it seems to have been fundamentally changed from what it was originally.

    There is visible proof that a significant change was made to the monument about 1750. (24) The proof is that we have a drawing from 1634 which confirms that the monument looked significantly different then than it does today.

    In July of 1634, the English antiquarian Sir William Dugdale visited Stratford and made a sketch of the monument as it then existed. This sketch later was found among his papers and was used as the model for the frontispiece for the 1709 collection of Shakespeare's works that was edited by Nicolas Rowe.

    Dugdale's sketch shows a dour man with long, drooping moustaches clutching an enormous sack. There can be no mistaking that, in the sketch, the subject of the memorial is clutching a sack. He does not hold a pen or a quill, and his hands are close together, as if he is exerting force on the sack, to hold it up or to clasp it to his bosom.

    Today, the effigy looks much different. Instead of a sack, the great poet's hands rest on a pillow or cushion. The hands are arranged as in the act of writing: the left hand rests upon a sheet of paper, which lies improbably on the pillow; the right hand seems to grip a non-existent pen.

    This is not to comment on the face with its vacuous eyes, its impertinent upward-pointing moustache, its expressionless mouth that is set in neither a smile nor a frown, that face that Mark Twain said possessed all the intelligence of a bladder. (25)

    Nor is it to point out that the face in the Stratford monument resembles neither the idiotic visage in the Droeshout engraving on the cover of the First Folio nor the ear-ringed thug whose countenance is captured in the Chandos Portrait.

    Why is the figure in today's Stratford monument appearing to write on a pillow?

44. Why did the antiquarian Sir William Dugdale in 1634 draw the same figure as if he were clutching an enormous sack of wool?

45. If Dugdale's sketch was accurate, then who was originally intended to be memorialized by the Stratford monument, William Shakespeare the poet and playwright, William Shakspere the malt horder or John Shakspere, the glover and wool merchant?

46. There are three pictorial representations of William Shakespeare that have any claim to authenticity. They are the Droeshout engraving, the Chandos Portrait and the bust in the Stratford memorial. In the first he looks like an idiot, in the second a thug, and in the third he looks like a fat and contented burgher. None of the three images resembles any of the others. How can it be that we do not know what the greatest poet in the English language looked like?

47. Why did the publishers of the *Mr. William Shakespeare's Comedies, Histories and Tragedies* (otherwise known as the First Folio, 1623) use an image of Jacobean poet Sir Thomas Overbury as the model for the engraving of the supposed author, William Shakespeare, which graces the cover of the book? (See Argument 43 in the following essay for the answer to this question.)

48. Some scholars, beginning with George Russell French in 1869, believe that the character of Polonius in *Hamlet* is a dramatic representation of William Cecil, Lord Burghley, who was Elizabeth's primary counselor, principal secretary and Lord Treasurer of England.

It is difficult to deny that there are striking similarities between Cecil and Polonius. Lord Burghley's book of advice to his son, *Certain Precepts*, which was published in 1618, contains numerous pithy maxims on how to advance one's career, which sound very much like the advice Polonius gives to Laertes in his "to thine own self be true" speech. Burghley's motto was "Cor unam, via una" (One heart, one way). In the 1603 version of *Hamlet,* (The Bad Quarto) the Polonius character is named Corambis (Two hearts), a very dexterous jab at Burghley's two-faced political instincts. When Burghley's son Thomas went to Paris to go to college, Burghley set underlings to spy on him; Polonius sets spies on Laertes and, of course, on Hamlet himself. In 1562, Lord Burghley got Parliament to pass a law making Wednesday a fast day, that is, the second day of the week on which the English people could eat fish, but not meat; Hamlet calls Polonius a "fishmonger."

These are only a few of the many parallels between Lord Burghley and Polonius in *Hamlet*. Accepting that Burghley was the model for Polonius, and remembering that *Certain Precepts* was published in 1618 but that *Hamlet* was published in 1603 and 1604, numerous questions arise. First, are we to assume that our playwright somehow had access to a manuscript version of the Lord Treasurer's advice to his son?

49. Failing the possibility that the manuscript of a recently deceased statesman could have fallen into his hands, how would Shakespeare have known that Lord Burghley wrote such an essay to his son?

50. Why would the existence of a meddlesome, loquacious prime minister get under the skin of a businessman-actor-playwright, who presumably had no contact with Queen Elizabeth's inner circle?

51. Or alternately, if Shakespeare did have contact and dealings with Queen Elizabeth's inner circle, how could that have happened?

52. Why would the author have pilloried Lord Burghley, not for public policy mistakes, but for family and personal reasons?

53. Why would a playwright, even a very good one, have dared to portray such a powerful man in such an unflattering light?

54. Within the English-speaking world, more books have been written about William Shakespeare than about any other person who ever lived. In fact, so many books have been written about Shakespeare that no one knows exactly how many. The best that can be done is to estimate the approximate scope of the field.

    Samuel Schoenbaum, in his 1971 book *Shakespeare's Lives*, examined 396 biographies and critical books about Shakespeare, spanning the centuries from 1640 to 1969. But Schoenbaum's review touched only the high points, and books that, from his perspective, represented the low points. It was nothing like exhaustive.

    Celestin Demblon, a Belgian professor who favored the Fifth Earl of Rutland as the author of the Works, is said to have read 5000 books on Shakespeare before writing his 1912 book, *Lord Rutland est Shakespeare*. (26) But 1912 was a century ago, and the argument about who Shakespeare was has been heating up since 1920 and certainly since 1980.

    James Shapiro, in his *Contested Will*, wrote that by 1949, more than 4,500 books had been written championing other candidates for the authorship of the Works. Shapiro wrote that since that year, scholars have given up counting how many of these types of books have been written. (27)

In the absence of better authority, I will estimate how many books on Shakespeare have been written to date. To do so, I will make three assumptions. The first assumption is that all books on Shakespeare, both critical and biographical, count. The second is that twice as many books have been written expounding, recounting or otherwise illuminating the life and/or work of Shakespeare, as have been written advancing the claims of some other candidate as the author. It could easily be more than two times, it could be four or ten, because for centuries the Stratford man was regarded as the greatest man who ever lived and, since no adequate biography had yet been, or could be, written about him, the lure of being the person to finally square the circle and explain Shakespeare was well nigh irresistible.

Also, for centuries Shakespeare's work has exerted a great claim on the imagination of the critically minded, and again, literally untold numbers of books have been written expounding on this or that aspect of the Works. But for the purposes of this calculation, I will use the very conservative number two: the number of books on the Stratford Shakespeare's life and works is twice the number of those that advance the claims of some other person as having been Shakespeare.

The second assumption I will make is that twenty percent as many books have been written supporting other candidates for the role of Shakespeare since 1950, as were written on that topic from 1850 to 1950. Again, this too is a very conservative number. It would seem that, if the authorship question has been heating up since 1950, more books taking that perspective will have been written over the past 60 years than during the first hundred years that the controversy had smoldered. But again, for the purposes of this calculation, I want to be conservative.

Taking then 4500 books as our starting point, and applying the second assumption, yields 900 "anti-Stratfordian" books written since 1950, giving a total of 5400 anti-Strat books since 1850. Then, using our first assumption, we get a subtotal of 10,800 books either critically assessing the works of Shakespeare or supporting or defending the theory that the man from Stratford was the author. The total number of books on Shakespeare is therefore probably in the range of 15,000 to 20,000 books.

We need also to keep in mind that these researchers have spent, literally, millions of hours researching Shakespeare. The early Twentieth Century American researchers Charles and Hulda Wallace looked through, by their own record, five million documents in search of clues about Shakespeare. (28) Charlotte Stopes, the biographer of the Third Earl of Southampton, spent eight years sifting through documents and letters in search of corroboration that the earl and Shakespeare knew each other. I am certain that many of the finest of Shakespearean scholars spent even more years than

Stopes, they spent their lives, looking for some clue or talisman that would explain Shakespeare to themselves and to the world.

That being said, if we accept that the man from Stratford was the author, to this day we know almost nothing about him. We know nothing about the lost years, nothing about his education, nothing about his supposed travels or his military experience, and, besides the fact that he was involved in a number of lawsuits over relatively small amounts of money, nothing about his retirement. We can only speculate as to what obscure and mysterious force in his life led him to imagine the agony of Hamlet and the pathos of King Lear, the self tortured ambition of Macbeth, the helpless fate of Romeo and Juliet. We can only guess about what led him to so unstintingly defend the aristocracy and to regard people from his own class as a gaggle of pathetic buffoons.

Writing in 1964, 400 years after Shakespeare's supposed birth, W.H. Auden summed up what we know about him, and his words ring as true today as they did when they were written. "Shakespeare is in the singularly fortunate position of being, to all intents and purposes, anonymous," he wrote. (29)

So the question is, after millions of hours of investigation by scholars and researchers, and after probably fifteen thousand books having been written about him, why do we still know so little about William Shakespeare?

55. As Oxfordian author J.T. Looney pointed out, when we consider the Works of William Shakespeare, and try to reasonably connect them with the life and career of William Shakspere, we are left with an insuperable conundrum. To be told that Shakespeare went from being a semi-literate schoolboy who dropped out of his town's grade school at age thirteen, who never went to college, who was raised by illiterate parents in a small, remote, backwater town where he lived until he was 21 or 22 years old, to becoming, in eight years, the author of *Venus and Adonis*, *The Rape of Lucrece*, and the astounding and varied body of the greatest dramatic literature in the history of the world, and then, to be further instructed that, at the age of 40, he returned to Stratford where, while continuing to write those plays, he pursued such activities as malt production and sales, money lending, real estate speculation and tax collection (with attendant litigation), until his death touched off, both locally in Stratford and nationally, a deafening crescendo of silence, defies logic and insults credulity. How could such a man have written the works of William Shakespeare?

NOTES

1. Greenblatt, Stephen. *Will In the World*, pg. 124.

2. Chute, Marchette. *Shakespeare of London*, pg. 135.

3. The assumption that he moved back to Stratford in 1604 is based on the fact that there are no records of his activities in London after 1604, until 1612, when he purchased a tenement apartment in the gatehouse of Blackfriars, a converted former monastery in London. During the same period (1604-1612), there are some few records of his activities in Stratford.

4. Moore, Peter. *The Lame Storyteller, Poor and Despised*. See the long essay "The Abysm of Time: the Chronology of Shakespeare's Plays," pages 159-199 in Moore's book; see pages 170-171 for the clearest statement of this view.

5. Whalen, Richard. "A Dozen Plays Written After Oxford Died? Not Proven!" *The Oxfordian, Volume 10*, (2007), pgs. 75-84.

6. Stritmatter, Roger, and Lynne Kositsky. "The Spanish Maze and the Date of The Tempest." *The Oxfordian, Volume 10*, 2007, pgs. 9-19.

7. Miller, Ruth Loyd. Oxfordian Vistas, (being Volume II of her 1975 edition of J.T. Looney's *Shakespeare Identified in Edward de Vere, Seventeenth Earl of Oxford*), page 280-283.

8. Ogburn, Charlton, Jr. *The Mysterious William Shakespeare*, second edition, 1992, pg. 112.)

9. *Ibid.*

10. Price, Diana. *Shakespeare's Unorthodox Biography*, pg. 59

11. Ogburn, op. cit., pg. 227.

12. Gilvary, Kevin. "Two Gentlmen of Verona: Italian literary traditions and the Authorship debate", *The Oxfordian, Volume VIII*, 2005, pgs. 76-92.

13. Whalen, Richard and Ren Dreya. Introduction to their edition of *Othello*, pg. 31. Published by Horation Editions, Lumina Press, 2010.

14. Gilvary, Kevin, op. cit. See especially Note 1, where Gilvary writes that Italian troupes performed in England in 1573, 1574 and 1576-1578, but not after that. Gilvary cites as his source Chambers, E.K., *The Elizabethan Stage, Vol. 2*, pg. 262

15. Ogburn, op. cit., pg. 730.

16. Greenblatt, Stephen, *Will in the World*, page 246.

17. Ogburn, Dorothy and Charlton, Sr., *This Star of England*, pg. 1241. The crucial quotation is, "Mrs. C.C. Stopes confessed that, in writing her biography of the Third Earl of Southampton, she spent eight years of industrious and painstaking research, ransacking the public records office, in the hope of finding some connection between Southampton and "Shakespeare" but found absolutely nothing; in consequence she felt that her life had been a failure."

18. Price, Diana, *Shakespeare's Unorthodox Biography*, pg. 254

19. Akgrigg, G.P.V., *Shakespeare and the Earl of Southampton*, pg. 193

20. Ogburn, Jr., op. cit., pg. 259

21. *Ibid.* pg. 320

22. *Ibid.* pg. 321

23. Chute, Marchette, pgs 343 and 344

24. Whalen, Richard F., "The Stratford Bust: A Monumental Fraud," *The Oxfordian*, Volume 8, 2005, pgs. 7-24

25. Twain, Mark *Is Shakespeare Dead?* Found on the Shakespeare Oxford Society website in the essay purporting to list all the verifiable facts about Shakespeare's life. Here is the marvelous quote in full: "… the precious bust, the priceless bust, the calm bust, the serene bust, with the dandy moustache, and the putty face, unseamed of care—that face which has looked passionlessly down upon the awed pilgrim for a hundred and fifty years and will still look down upon the awed pilgrim three hundred more, with the deep deep deep, subtle subtle subtle, expression of a bladder…."

26. Michell, John. *Who Wrote Shakespeare?*, pg. 9

27. Shapiro, James. *Contested Will*, pg. 2

28. Schoenbaum, Stephen. *Shakespeare's Lives*, 1971 edition, pg. 648

29. Auden, W.H. page xix of his introduction to the Signet Classic edition of *The Sonnets* (1964).

FORTY-EIGHT ARGUMENTS IN FAVOR OF EDWARD DE VERE AS THE AUTHOR OF THE WORKS OF WILLIAM SHAKESPEARE

> "I think Oxford wrote Shakespeare. If you don't agree, there
> are some awfully funny coincidences to explain away."
> Orson Welles

(*Note*: Although much is known about Edward de Vere, the truth about his parentage is, at this time, still in dispute. I believe that the most outrageous and incredible of family histories is true in his case and that the standard model of his family story is false.

However, I wish to focus in this essay exclusively on offering arguments for why Edward de Vere is the author of the Works of William Shakespeare. Therefore, I will take the conventional view, that his parents were John de Vere, the 16th Earl of Oxford, and Margery Golding Vere, Countess of Oxford. The real identity of his parents will be explored in the next essay.

Also, the names Oxford, the Earl of Oxford and Edward de Vere are used interchangeably. As is customary with Oxfordian writers, the name Shakespeare is used to identify the author of the Works, the name Shakspere is used to identify the man from Stratford.)

1. The author of the Works must have belonged to the nobility, because the point of view expressed in the plays is always aristocratic.

    Shakespeare was obsessed with good government and with creating and maintaining a strong social order. Again and again, his plays ask, what is it that gives a kingdom to one man and not another? What happens to the state when a poor ruler is on the throne? What is it that the nobility owes to the sovereign? What do the people—the common people—owe to the state? What does the sovereign owe to the state and to the people?

    At the same time, the common people are always disparaged. They are buffoons and servants, messengers and pages, bawds and barmaids. The idea that they should have or could have a better life is almost never broached.

The author of the plays, therefore, must have been of the upper classes or the nobility.

Edward de Vere was the 17th Earl of Oxford, the seventeenth earl in a long line of one of the oldest, most respected, wealthiest and most powerful families in England. The First Earl of Oxford was confirmed in that title in 1142.

The British Victorian historian Thomas Babington Macaulay wrote that the Veres were "the longest and most illustrious line of nobles that England has seen, whose heads brought it honor in the fields of Hastings, Jerusalem, Runnymeade, Crecy, Poitiers, Bosworth and the Court of Elizabeth, where shone the 17th Earl who had won himself an honorable place among the early masters of English poetry."

De Vere's life was touched by contact with poets of a very high quality. De Vere's aunt, Frances Vere, was the wife of Henry Howard, Earl of Surrey. Surrey was certainly among the best and most influential poets of the preceding generation, that is, the later years of the reign of Henry VIII. Surrey contributed forty poems to *The Book of Songs and Sonnets* (also called *Tottle's Miscellany*.) He was the first English poet to write in the English sonnet form—four quatrains and a couplet: abab cdcd efef gg, the form that later came to be called the Shakespearean sonnet. He was also the first poet to publish English poetry in blank verse. Thus, he invented the two most famous and most widely used poetic modes in all of English poetry.

Howard was beheaded for pseudo-treasonous actions in 1547, in one of the last actions of the very paranoid Henry VIII. Having such an illustrious poet in the family may have had an effect on Oxford as a youth.

Also, the most famous translator of the period, Arthur Golding, was de Vere's uncle. He was the half-brother of Margery Golding, de Vere's mother. Arthur Golding is best known as the translator into English of Ovid's *Metamorphoses*, which was arguably the most influential and most popular book of poetry published in 16th Century England.

From 1562 to 1571, de Vere was a ward of the crown. He was raised under the protection and direction of Queen Elizabeth in the household of William Cecil, Lord Burghley. William Cecil was Principal Secretary to Elizabeth and later, Lord Treasurer of England. Because of the influence that Burghley had with Elizabeth and with other powerful statesmen, Lord Burghley was the most powerful man in England.

Therefore, de Vere was born to the most ancient and respected of noble families in England, educated and raised by one of the greatest scholars in the country and then "finished" by the Principal Secretary to the Queen herself. De Vere's aristocratic background is consonant with the life and position of the man who would have written the Works of William Shakespeare.

2. De Vere's education is consonant with the education likely required by the author of the the Works.

    De Vere received an excellent education, probably the best that could be obtained in the England of his time. As a child he was raised in the home of Sir Thomas Smith, one of the leading scholars in England. Smith had been provost at Eton College, was the Chair of Civil Law at Cambridge University, was a fine teacher and pedagogue, an economist, a student of plants, gardening and herbal medicine, and a poet, albeit one who wrote in Greek.

    Sir Thomas Smith served his country in politics as well, and was Secretary of State under Edward VI in the late 1540s and again to Elizabeth in the 1570s. He was ambassador to France several times, one of the most important positions in the realm. His biographer writes "he bore a great part, both in the university, the church and the commonwealth."

    Oxford entered Queen's College, Cambridge University in November 1558. He stayed there for some time, but we know nearly nothing about his academic career there. After the death of his father (1562) he went to live in London with William Cecil, Lord Burghley, who saw to his education. De Vere was tutored privately by several talented scholars, including Lawrence Nowell and possibly Arthur Golding. Burghley possessed one of the finest and most extensive libraries in England, which included numerous rare and foreign language books that later scholars have concluded would have been source material for the author of the Works.

    In 1564, de Vere received an honorary bachelor's degree from Cambridge University. In 1566, he received an honorary master's degree from Oxford University. In 1567, de Vere attended Gray's Inn, where he studied law.

    So concludes de Vere's formal education. His education was sufficient to provide the basis in knowledge for the author of the Works.

3. There is abundant evidence that Edward de Vere was regarded in his own day as an excellent writer. However, his works—except for two dozen short lyrical poems—have been lost to us.

    In 1578, de Vere accompanied Queen Elizabeth to Cambridge University. The Queen's party stopped off at Audley End, home of the Earl of Leicester, where an academic named Gabriel Harvey read a round of Latin encomia to the greatness of the Queen and her glittering court. Of de Vere, Harvey wrote, in Latin:

    > Thy splendid fame, great earl,
    > demands even more than in the case of others
    > the services of a poet possessing lofty eloquence.

Thy merit does not creep along the ground,
nor can it be confined within the limits of a song.
It is a wonder which reaches as far
as the heavenly orbs. . . .
For a long time past
Phoebus Apollo has cultivated thy
mind in the arts. English poetical measure
have been sung by thee long enough.
. . . . I have seen many Latin verses of thine,
yes, even more English verses are extant.
Thou hast drunk deep draughts
not only of the muses of France and Italy,
but hast learned the manners of many men
and the arts of foreign countries.

So at least in court circles, de Vere was famous as a writer by 1578.

In 1585, William Webbe wrote in a published book titled *Discourse On English Poetry* about the Earl of Oxford's "splendid fame."

"I may not omit the deserved commendations of many honorable lords and gentlemen in Her Majesty's court, which, in devices of poetry, have been and yet are the most skillful, among whom the Right Honorable Earl of Oxford may challenge to himself the title of the most excellent among the rest."

In 1589, an author, (variously reported to be either Lord Lumley or Sir George Puttenham) wrote about de Vere in *The Art of English Poetry*:

"And in Her Majesty's time that now is are sprung up another crew of courtly makers, noblemen and gentlemen of Her Majesty's own servants, who have written commendably well—as it would appear if their doings could be found out and made public with the rest—of which number is first that noble gentleman, Edward, Earl of Oxford."

In 1598, Francis Meres wrote in *Palladis Tamia* that "the best for comedy among us be Edward Earle of Oxford." He then went on to list others who were notable for their comedic writings.

In 1622, in his critical look at contemporary English society titled *The Complete Gentleman*, Henry Peacham named Edward de Vere first in his list of accomplished Elizabethan poets, and failed to even mention William Shakespeare.

This occurs in his chapter on English poetry, in which he first mentions the great or notable poets of England's past: Geoffry Chaucer, Gower, Ludgate, Harding, Skelton, the Earl of Surrey and Sir Thomas Wyatt, among others.

Then Peacham praises the reign of Elizabeth. He calls it "a golden age" for poetry, and notes that it produced poets "whose like are hardly to be hoped for in any succeeding age."

He then offers his list of the finest of Elizabethan poets: "Edward Earl of Oxford, the Lord Buckhurst, Henry Lord Paget, the noble Sir Philip Sidney, M. Edward Dyer, M. Edmund Spenser, Master Samuel Daniel, with sundry others whom (together with those admirable wits yet living and so well known) not out of envy, but to avoid tediousness, I overpass."

Recall *The Complete Gentleman* was published in 1622, six years after the death of William Shakspere and 18 years after the death of Edward de Vere. Why did he mention Edward de Vere, who had not published any books of poetry under his name for a half century, and whose lyrical poems, though they are fine examples of early Elizabethan poetry, hardly would entitle him to be ranked above Marlowe and Spenser? Why did he not mention William Shakespeare, who presumably would have been at least noticed in any catalogue of notable English poets?

4. Edward de Vere had documented contact with the leading writers and personalities of his day.

First of all we note that de Vere had a personal acquaintance with Queen Elizabeth and that he spent most of his time at court from the years 1570 to 1580. Therefore, in addition to Elizabeth, he would have known both the major and the minor players of English politics: Leicester, Burghley, Walsingham, Robert Cecil, Christopher Hatton and the Earl of Sussex, among others.

We have already noted de Vere's relationship with Arthur Golding, the translator of Ovid's *Metamorphoses*. Beginning in 1579, de Vere's secretary John Lyly published two novels which became the most popular novels in the England of the time: *Euphues, the Anatomy of Wit*, (1579) and *Euphues, His England* (1580). These are thought to be the second and third novels in the English language. As with other Oxfordian writers, I must point out that, while Lyly was in the employ of de Vere, he wrote original and important work; after leaving de Vere's employ he wrote nothing.

A third notable literary connection is that between Edmund Spenser and de Vere. There is little historical evidence documenting the extent and depth of their friendship; however, Spenser did include a dedicatory poem to de Vere in the first edition of *The Faery Queen*. It is believed by many Oxfordian scholars that Spenser refers to de Vere several times throughout his poetry. For example, in the *The Shepherd's Calendar* (1579) , Spenser writes of a poetic duel between bucolic poets Willie and Perigot. These are thought to be de Vere, who is Willie, and Perigot, who is Sir Philip Sidney. (1)

Also in *The Tears of the Muses* (1592), Spenser laments the quiescence of a poet he refers to as "pleasant Willie."

> And he the man whom Nature's self had made
> to mock herself and truth to imitate,
> with kindly counter under mimic shade,
> our pleasant Willie, ah! is dead of late,
> with whom all joy and jolly merriment
> is also deaded and in doleur drent.

> But that same gentle spirit from whose pen
> large streams of honey and sweet nectar flow,
> scorning the boldness of such base-born men,
> which dare their follies forth so rashly throw,
> doeth rather chose to sit in idle cell
> than so himself to mockery to sell.

A fourth important literary contact with de Vere is Philip Sidney. The two men quarreled over who took precedence on the tennis court (1579), they were "the poets" of two rival political factions, de Vere being associated (albeit unhappily) with the Cecils and Sidney more congenially with Leicester; they were rivals for the hand of Anne Cecil (1569-1571), and they became the leaders of two rival groups of writers.

In fact, de Vere knew nearly all of the leading personalities of his day. A brief passage by Oxfordian biographer Joseph Sobran sums it up well.

"With remarkable frequency, then, Oxford's life touches the lives of personalities familiar to students of Shakespeare: Elizabeth I, Golding, Burghley, Harvey, Lyly, Sidney, Watson, Greene, Nashe, Southampton, Spenser, Munday, Derby, Chapman, Meres, Raleigh, Essex, James I, Pembroke, Montgomery.

"Of course, it was a smaller world—London, including the suburbs, contained only 200,000 people. The world of the theatre, with no more than four acting companies existing at a time, was even smaller—which only makes it extremely incongruous that this great patron of the theatre, living in London from the 1590s to his death in 1604, never seems to have crossed paths with William Shakespeare." (2)

5. The author of the Works appears to have had a cavalier attitude toward money. That attitude is matched by that of Edward de Vere.

We would expect for William Shakespeare to have had a liberal attitude toward money. He is our foremost poet of love, (*Romeo and Juliet* and the sonnets); he is our foremost poet also of the individual suffering at the hands of society (*Hamlet*) and at the hands of fate (*King Lear*). In the plays, he seems to be saying that what people need is satisfied romantic love, we need a just

society based on living in truth (*Hamlet*) and we need compassi˚
people and for ourselves (*King Lear*). Money doesn't figure
in his calculations.

De Vere had a very liberal attitude toward money. He was a patron to poets, writers, artists, musicians. Twenty eight books were dedicated to him during his life. He sold 55 of his father's 78 estates in order to finance his literary and theatrical ventures. (3)

In April, 1571, de Vere received his liberty from his wardship. At that time, he was "fined" £3306 for his wardship. (In 2009 American dollars, $1.26 million.) In other words, he had to pay £3306 in order to free himself from debt to the crown; the "debt" was the amount of money that the crown had spent in raising him. If a newly freed ward didn't pay, a fine would be added to the total.

This is what happened to Edward de Vere: he repeatedly failed to pay even the interest on his debt and it grew for a dozen years, swelling to £14,754 ($3.9 million) by 1583. (4) There is no record or indication that de Vere ever worried about money or made any kind of concerted effort to pay off his debt, or even to pay off part of it.

Indeed, in his later years, he attempted to sell his lands to third parties, when he knew those lands were already encumbered with debt. Apparently, he did not put much value upon money, so long as it was available. "Spend it all" might well have been his motto.

De Vere's attitude toward money corresponds much more to William Shakespeare's than does that of William Shakspere, who sued his neighbors over relatively small amounts, evaded the tax collector in London for several years, whose property in his room in London was assessed at a value of £5 in October 1596 (5), and who is known to have hoarded grain during a famine in Stratford.

6. De Vere's travels provide the kind of detailed, first-hand knowledge of continental Europe that the author of the Works would be presumed to have had.

William Shakespeare very likely traveled on the continent, because the author of the Works sets many of his plays in Italy and France. Moreover, several researchers have concluded that the author of the Works exhibits first-hand knowledge of the geography and customs of continental Europe, especially Italy and France. It is difficult to imagine how the Stratford man could have afforded a trip to the continent in his formative years. There is no record of his having traveled there after 1593.

Edward de Vere traveled on the continent at least twice: in 1574 for a month, and from January 1575 to April 1576. During the second, longer trip he visited Germany, France and Italy; he made his headquarters in Venice.

7. A few details from the travels of de Vere seem to strongly suggest episodes in the plays.

    Only a few details of his journey have come down to us. We do know, however, that on the return trip, while he was traveling up the Rhone Valley in France, he was offered an opportunity to review the troops of the German Duke Jon Casimir, who had invaded France and was preparing to overthrow the government with the collusion of the French Protestant faction. De Vere refused to review Casimir's troops.

8. Then, as he was crossing the channel on the homeward leg, a few weeks after refusing to review Casimir's troops, he was attacked by pirates. They stripped him, robbed him, and only spared his life at the last moment. In *Hamlet*, Hamlet is also attacked by pirates. (IV, 6) The attack occurs just after he has reviewed Fortinbras' troops. (IV, 4).

9   De Vere was aided financially by two men during this trip. One was Baptista Nigrone, who loaned him 500 crowns to continue his trip when he was in Padua. The other was Baptista Spinola, a Marrano Jew living in London, who loaned de Vere money through his business representative in Venice.

    In the plays, Kate's father in *The Taming of the Shrew* is named Baptista Minola. In *Much Ado About Nothing*, one of the central characters is named Benedict Spinole.

10. De Vere's sojourn in Italy would explain Shakespeare's knowledge of many Italian customs and points of geography.

    One example of this is Shakespeare's apparent belief that people considered inland cities in Italy, such as Milan and Verona, as port cities. Shakespeare, in *Two Gentlemen of Verona*, has characters who are living in Verona speak of traveling to Milan by boat. Critics have for centuries derided Shakespeare for these "mistakes", claiming that the Bard was inattentive to detail, especially in his plays set in Italy.

    In fact, travel by river was a normal and even a preferred mode of traveling in Italy from Roman times. In the Middle Ages, a system of canals was added in the northern region of Lombardy, so that river travel became commonplace. The inland city of Verona became known as La Porta d'Italia, or the Gateway to Italy. It was possible to travel, as Valentine does in *Two Gentlemen of Verona*, from Verona to Milan by boat, without sailing on the Mediterranean.

    This fact would be difficult to obtain by a man who most likely never left

England, as we suppose Will Shakspere must have been. But it would have easily been assimilated by someone who actually traveled in Italy, on some occasions by boat, as was common in those days.

11. Rosalind's jest seems to express what de Vere did in his own life.

In January 1575, Edward de Vere left London for an extended tour of the continent. He was gone for 14 months; during which time he spent £4,561 or about $1.6 million. In order to finance his trip, he had to borrow money from creditors; he also directed Lord Burghley to sell one or more of his ancestral estates.

In *As You Like It* (IV, 3), Rosalind tells Jacques,

> "I fear you have sold your own lands to see
> other men's; then to have seen much and to have
> nothing is to have rich eyes and poor hands.

This is exactly what de Vere did: he "sold his own lands to see other men's."

12. William Shakespeare was very familiar with Ovid. He quotes him in nearly every play and numerous story ideas and classical references are drawn from Ovid's writings. The translator of Ovid's greatest poem, *The Metamorphoses*, has for centuries been thought to be Arthur Golding, who was Edward de Vere's uncle and who lived with and worked for William Cecil, Lord Burghley, during the period that Edward de Vere was living in Cecil House.

I believe that Edward de Vere was the author of Golding's translation of Ovid's *Metamorphoses*. I come to this conclusion because Golding was quite unlike Ovid in disposition, taste and religious view. Golding was a Puritan with a love of history and religious tracts. He translated 22 works, including histories by Trogus Pompeius and Julius Caesar and ten books on Christian subjects, including five books by John Calvin. Other than *The Metamorphoses*, Golding translated no secular poetry. It is quite strange that he would have been drawn to translate Ovid, whose theme, the cavortings and love affairs of the gods and goddesses and the creation of the phenomenological world as the whimsical result of those cavortings, would have been anathema to the Puritan translator of John Calvin.

A study of his work as a translator, focusing on the likely time frame during which the work was done, shows that while working on Ovid, he was working on two major works at the same time. Not impossible, but unlike his work habits at other times in his life. (6)

Close analysis of Golding's translation work shows that, in all of his translation work except for *The Metamorphoses*, he is extremely faithful to the original, adding no extra words of his own. In the case of *The Metamorphoses* he abandons this principle, and adds more than 2500 lines to Ovid's original 12,000 lines. (7)

This anomalous blip in Golding's work habits—translating two major works simultaneously, freely adding more words and lines to the original, coining new words, dashing off lines of true poetry, dealing with non-religious and non-Christian themes, can be explained. The work was done by his nephew, Edward de Vere, and was given to the world as his own.

Even if this theory is wrong and Arthur Golding was the real translator of Ovid's *Metamorphoses*, it is quite easy to imagine that the uncle would have introduced the young literary earl to the glories of the pagan poet while both were living under the roof of William Cecil.

13. The Earl of Oxford experienced a lifetime of social rejection and shame. This comports well with the tenor of some of the sonnets.

In his youth he dressed and spent extravagantly. In his late twenties he was called "The Italianate Earl" due to his affectation of Italian fashion. During the same period he was described in print as riding his horse along the London streets while veiling his face, presumably to keep the sun and wind from spoiling his complexion.

He squandered the patrimony of his father, the 16th Earl of Oxford, in order to finance his travels, his theatre companies, and to support other poets, scholars, musicians and writers.

He published his poetry under his own name in the early 1570s, which was not considered a proper thing for a member of the nobility to do. He was the patron of at least two theatre companies: Oxford's Boys and Oxford's Men. Being associated with the theatre carried with it a stigma, particularly for the upper classes. Because he did these things, he would have been reviled by many members of his own class.

He omitted to pay the fees from his wardship, instead letting the interest and fines for nonpayment swell his debt to £14,754.

He was a poor husband to his first wife, Anne Cecil. He publicly stated that he rarely or never had sexual relations with her. Then, after she had given birth to their first daughter, he denied paternity of the child and abandoned the Countess, forcing her to live for five years the life of a spinster in her father's house.

In March 1581, Anne Vavasor, a Gentlewoman of the Queen's Bedchamber, gave birth to a son, and confessed that the father of the child was de Vere. Elizabeth threw father, mother and son into the Tower. She then separated the mother and son from de Vere and banished him from court for two years.

When Anne Cecil died, he did not attend her funeral. Soon thereafter he was judged to be an unfit parent and his three daughters were taken from him and sent to live with Lord Burghley.

When taking this life history into account, we can easily imagine that at some point he may have been tempted to write:

> When in disgrace with fortune and men's eyes
> I all alone beweep my outcast state...
> Sonnet 29

14. The life situation of de Vere bears an impressive degree of similarity to the protagonist's situation in *Hamlet*.

    John de Vere, the 16th Earl of Oxford and Edward de Vere's father, died suddenly, just a few days after writing and signing his third will, in early August, 1562. The man who, by arrangements encoded in the will, received all of John de Vere's extensive holdings, was Robert Dudley, Earl of Leicester. Leicester was Elizabeth's Master of Horse, companion, friend, and lover. He was notorious for having poisoned numerous people in his life. He seemed to leave a trail of blood and death wherever he went.

    Also, de Vere's mother, Margery Golding, married Charles Tyrell, a lieutenant of Robert Dudley's, just a few months after John de Vere's death. The date of their marriage is not known; however, she wrote of them as being a couple in October 1563, within 14 months of his death.

    Therefore, assuming that John de Vere's sudden death was by poison and that the perpetrator was Leicester, we see a striking parallel: Edward de Vere's father was poisoned by the Queen's lover, Leicester, the man who was most like the king in the kingdom; and his mother, Margery Golding, married Leicester's henchman soon after. In *Hamlet*, of course, Prince Hamlet's father has been killed by his father's brother, Claudius, who marries Queen Gertrude within months of the dead king's funeral.

15. But there's more. Beginning with George Russell French (1869), some scholars have believed that the character of Polonius in *Hamlet* was patterned on Lord Burghley. A few reasons here must suffice to explain why this identification is certain.

    a)   In 1562, Lord Burghley got Parliament to pass a law making Wednesday another fast day. The people could eat no meat, but they could eat fish. Burghley reportedly pushed this bill in order to expand the country's fishing fleet and at the same time to strengthen England's navy. In the play, Hamlet calls Polonius a "fishmonger."

b)   Burghley told the world that he was born during the Diet of Worms; after Hamlet slays Polonius, he tells Claudius that

> "A certain convocation of politic worms
> are e'en at him. Your worm is your only
> emperor for diet. ..." *Hamlet*, IV, 3

c)   Burghley's motto was "Cor unam, via una" (One heart, one way); in the 1603 bad quarto of *Hamlet*, the name of the Polonius character is Corambis (Two hearts or Double-Hearted) a not-so-subtle jab at a hypocritical or duplicitous politician.

d)   In the play, Polonius sends spies to spy on his son, Laertes (II, 1). Lord Burghley had one of the most extensive spy networks in England. He spied on his own sons and on de Vere.

e)   Burghley was proud of his connection to Cambridge University, where he had gone as a youth, and where he was chancellor throughout his life. In *Hamlet* (III, 2) Polonius tells Hamlet that he had once acted in a play at the university.

f)   Burghley was not known as a lover, but, in his youth, he did marry for love and against his parents' wishes, when he married Mary Cheke, "in secret."

In *Hamlet*, Polonius also admits to having loved passionately in his youth:

"Truly in my youth I suffered much extremity for love, very near this." (II, 2)

g)   In Gabriel Harvey's address to various nobles and courtiers which he gave at Audley End in 1578, he refers to Burghley three times as "Polus." J. Valcourt Miller writes that "The Latin definition of 'Polus' is 'the end of an axle around which the wheel turns' or 'that around which the heavens turn.'" (8) Polus is suggestive of Polonius.

h)   William Cecil wrote a book of maxims intended to instruct one or both of his sons on how to live. The pamphlet was published in 1618, twenty years after Burghley's death, and titled *Certain Precepts or Directions*. Comparison between examples from *Certain Precepts* and from Polonius' advice to Laertes (*Hamlet*, I, 3) is striking.

From *Certain Precepts*:

> "Let thy hospitality be moderate. . . . rather plentiful than sparing, for I never knew any man grow poor by keeping an ordinary table. ... Beware thou spendest not more than three of four parts of thy revenue, and not above a third part of that in thy house. That gentleman who sells an acre of land sells an ounce of credit, for gentility is

nothing else but ancient riches. Suffer not thy sons to cross the Alps, for they shall learn nothing there but pride, blasphemy, and atheism; and if by travel they get a few broken languages, they shall profit them nothing more than to have one meat served up in divers dishes. Neither train them up in war, for he that sets up to live by that profession can hardly be an honest man or a good Christian. Beware of being surety for thy best friends; he that payeth another man's debts seeketh his own decay. Be sure to keep some great man thy friend, but trouble him not with trifles; compliment him often with many, yet small, gifts, and of little charge. And if thou hast cause to bestow any great gratuity, let it be something which may be daily in sight.

Otherwise, in this ambitious age, thou shalt remain like a hop without a pole, live in obscurity and be made a football for every insulting companion to spurn at. Towards thy superiors be humble yet generous; with thine equals familiar yet respective; towards thine inferiors show much humanity and some familiarity, as to bow the body, stretch forth the hand and uncover the head, with such like popular accomplishments. The first prepares the way to advancement. The second makes thee known for a man well bred. The third gains a good report which, once got, is easily kept. For right humanity takes such deep root in the minds of the multitude, as they are easlier gained by unprofitable courtesies than by churlish benefits. Yet I advise thee not to affect, or neglect, popularity too much. Seek not to be Essex, shun to be Raleigh."

Compare the above lines with Polonius's advice to Laertes (*Hamlet*, I, 3).

> There—my blessing with thee,
> And these few precepts in thy memory
> Look thou character. Give thy thoughts no tongue,
> Nor any unproportioned thought his act.
> Be thou familiar but by no means vulgar.
> Those friends thou hast and their adoption tried,
> grapple them to thy soul with hoops of steel;
> but do not dull thy palm with entertainment
> of each new-hatched, unfledged comrade. Beware
> of entrance to a quarrel, but, being in,
> bear't that the opposed may beware of thee.
> Give every man thy ear, but few thy voice;
> Take each man's censure, but reserve thy judgment.
> Costly thy habit as thy purse can buy,
> But not expressed in fancy; rich, not gaudy,
> For the apparel oft proclaims the man,
> And they in France of the best rank and station

> Are of a most select and generous, chief in that.
> Neither a borrower nor a lender be,
> For loan oft loses both itself and friend,
> And borrowing dulls the edge of husbandry.
> This above all, to thine own self be true,
> And it must follow, as the day the night,
> Thou canst not then be false to any man.

These few connections will I hope demonstrate that whoever wrote *Hamlet* had Lord Burghley in mind for the character of Polonius. This view is supported by George Russell French (1869), Lilian Winstanley (1920) and Joel Hurstfield (1958).

16. But there is still more. In December 1571, Edward de Vere married Anne Cecil, the daughter of William Cecil. Their marriage was difficult, irregular and unhappy, for Edward apparently did not love her and was not attracted to her physically—or politically, which in his case was a major consideration.

    Scholarship has demonstrated that Edward was, for the first ten years of their marriage, a thoroughly rotten husband to Anne Cecil de Vere. He spent very little time with his wife and, by his own account, only slept with her one time during the first three years of their marriage. (9) Then, he traveled without her to the continent and stayed there for 14 months. Upon his return, in April 1576, he concluded that a daughter born during his absence (officially in July 1575 but possibly in September 1575) could not be his, and separated from her for five years.

    He finally returned to her in December 1581. Anne Cecil bore three more daughters and a son; the son died in infancy and one of the three daughters, Frances, died before her fourth birthday. Anne Cecil died in 1588 at the age of 32.

17. De Vere had family contacts that would have informed him about customs in the Danish Court, which are referred to in *Hamlet*.

    In 1582, Oxford's brother in law, Peregrine Bertie, Lord Willoughby d'Eresby, was given an embassage to the court of the Danish king at Elsinore Castle, Denmark. Bertie was directed by Elizabeth to invest King Frederick II of Denmark as a Knight of the Garter. Bertie was also instructed to negotiate with Frederick to tell the Danish navy to stop interfering with English ships.

    Between 1582 and 1585, Bertie spent five months at Elsinore. He met one Danish courtier named Rosenkranz and two surnamed Guildenstern. He was also feted in a particularly Danish style. "The Danish king feted Bertie with multiple nights of revelry that included grand speeches about Her Majesty and the Order of the Garter." (8) Willoughby summarized his embassy in a handwritten manuscript that he circulated at court. In his own words, he stated that these speeches took place "after a whole volley of all the great shot of the castle discharged."

Hamlet chronicles this particularly Danish drinking ritual.

> "There's no health the king shall drink today
> but the great cannon to the clouds shall tell."
> says King Claudius.

18. Edward de Vere's cousins, Horace (or Horatio) Vere and Sir Francis Vere, were famous soldiers of the era. They were known as "the Fighting Veres." Both of them fought in the campaign in the Netherlands, from 1585 to 1604 (for Sir Francis) and from 1590 to 1632 (for Horatio) and both assumed various types of command, Francis serving as general of the English forces (about 1600) and Horace serving as colonel of the English forces after 1604, when the peace with Spain had been declared. Both men served as military governor of the Brielle and both are buried in Westminster Abbey. (11) In Hamlet, Francisco is a soldier and Horatio is Hamlet's best friend.

To conclude our argument regarding *Hamlet*, Edward de Vere's life situation closely parallels that of Hamlet. His father has been murdered by the man who sleeps with the Queen; his mother has speedily been remarried to that man's lieutenant, he is beset and spied upon by the Queen's chief counselor and he is in an unhappy romantic relationship with the daughter of that same counselor. In addition, de Vere's brother-in-law went on a diplomatic mission to Elsinore Castle, where he met two diplomats named Rosenkrantz and Guildenstern and learned that members of the Danish court had an unusually intense way of drinking. *Hamlet* is autobiographical.

19. Scholars have illuminated a link between the old Anglo-Saxon poem *Beowulf* and *Hamlet*. This link has no causal explanation in the case of William of Stratford, but does have a causal explanation in the case of the Earl of Oxford.

For centuries, scholars have known two sources for *Hamlet*: Saxo Grammaticus's *Historiae Danicae* and its 1570 translation (into French) by Belleforest as *Histoires Tragiques*. But some have noticed that neither of these two works provide a model for the very end of *Hamlet*, after the protagonist has killed his uncle.

In 1990, such a model was located in *Beowulf*. In that poem, after Beowulf (who at the end of the poem is an old man) has slain his final dragon and lies dying, he asks his faithful steward, Wiglaf, to attend to his funeral.

> Have the brave Gaets build me a tomb.
> When the funeral flames have burned me,
> and build it here,

at the water's edge,
high on this spit of land, so sailors
can see this tower and remember my name,
and call it Beowulf's tower,
and boats in the darkness and mist,
crossing the sea,
will know it.

Then that brave king gave the golden
necklace from around his throat to Wiglaf,
gave him his gold-covered helmet, and his rings,
and his mail shirt, and ordered him
to use them well;

You're the last of our far-flung family,
fate has swept our race away,
taken warriors in their strength and led them
to the death that was waiting. And now I follow them.

The old man's mouth was silent, spoke
no more, had said as much as it could.
He would sleep in the fire, soon. His soul
left his flesh, flew to glory.

Andrew Hannas, the scholar who first noticed *Beowulf*'s similarity to *Hamlet*, summarizes the similarities. "In the dying words of Hamlet we see a refiguring of the poignant exchange between the dying Beowulf and his faithful (and lone follower) Wiglaf—who is also a relative, a cousin, of his lord. Not insignificantly, both Beowulf and Hamlet are concerned not just about their own names and stories—which Wiglaf and Horatio will report—but also over the fate of the kingdom, the succession to the throne. Both lands either are or soon will be overrun by a foreign power. And oddly, the puzzling slipping of time, the aging of Beowulf bears a curious resemblance to the passage of time in which Hamlet appears in Act V to have aged from a prince in early manhood to an ostensible thirty years of age."

The question now becomes, if there is a connection between *Beowulf* and *Hamlet*, how can we account for it? Doing so is difficult in the case of William of Stratford, because only one manuscript of the poem was known to exist in the world between the years 1000 and 1787.

In the case of the Earl of Oxford, an explanation becomes possible, because, remarkably, that one manuscript fell into the hands of William Cecil's employee and Oxford's tutor, Lawrence Nowell, in 1563. Nowell was a pioneer in Anglo-Saxon studies and one of the first collectors of Old English manuscripts in England. In 1563 he received a collection of manuscripts written in the Old English hand, which later became known as the Nowell Codex. Among those manuscripts was the world's only known copy of the poem *Beowulf*.

Nowell must have shared his ancient manuscript with his brilliant pupil. The proof of that conjecture lies in the demonstrated similarity between the endings of *Beowulf* and *Hamlet*. (12)

20. In *3 Henry VI*, Shakespeare portrayed John de Vere, the 13th Earl of Oxford, in a very flattering light. According to J.T. Looney, "he is hardly mentioned except to be praised," and Looney gives as examples the following mentions of Oxford:

> "And thou, brave Oxford, wondrous well-beloved"
> "Sweet Oxford"
> "Oxford, Oxford, for Lancaster"
> "O welcome Oxford, for we want thy help"
> "Why, is not Oxford here another anchor?" (13)

The 13th earl becomes a symbol for the whole House of Lancaster when, in *Richard III*, King Edward remembers that Clarence was the one who saved him "on the field of Tewksbury, when Oxford had me down."

Looney continues to follow the glorification of John de Vere in *Richard III*. "In the last act of all, when the Yorkists are overthrown and Henry Tudor appears, it is with Oxford by his side, and it is Oxford who, as premier nobleman, replies first to the king's address to his followers." (14)

From this we gather that Shakespeare, whoever he was, was careful to portray at least one earl of Oxford in a flattering light.

21. On the other hand, in one instance when it would be presumed that an unsavory character, who happened to be an earl of Oxford, would have been given a role in a Shakespeare play, he was not.

This was Robert de Vere, the 9th Earl of Oxford, who lived from 1362 to 1392, and who was the favorite of King Richard II. Richard gave Robert numerous titles, lands and offices, including Chamberlain, Lord Great Chamberlain, member of the Privy Council, Knight of the Garter, Chief Justice of Chester, Justice of North Wales, Marquis of Dublin and Duke of Ireland. The two men were said to be inseparable.

"His elevation caused much resentment especially among the older nobility and the king's ambitious uncles such as Thomas of Woodstock, Duke of Gloucester. His reputation was not enhanced by his role in the Scottish expedition (1385), which was a fiasco, and by his divorce (1387) and marriage to the Bohemian Agnes Lancecrona. ... In the 1380s he was constantly under attack by the nobility and commons for leading the king astray, but there is no evidence that his influence was vicious; he merely lacked ability and judgment, which in the circumstances of the day, was disastrous." (15)

On December 20, 1387, near Witney in Oxfordshire, Robert was leading the royal army against the armies of his usurping uncles. Oxford lost control of his troops, which broke up in disarray. When pressed by the onslaught of the enemy, he abandoned the field, crossed the Thames (either on horseback or by swimming) and doubled back to London, disguised as a groom. He fled to Flanders.

His lands, titles and possessions were taken from him by Parliament in 1388 and he spent the last five years of his life living in penury. Like Adonis in Shakespeare's poem *Venus and Adonis,* he died while hunting, gored to death by a wild boar.

As King Richard's closest friend and ally and as one whom many blamed for the king's errant politics and subsequent downfall, Robert de Vere should have been given a major role in Shakespeare's play *Richard II.* Yet he is not a character in that play. In fact, he is mentioned only one time, in the quarto edition as having been executed for supporting the king. In the First Folio, the name Spencer is substituted for that of Oxford, so that, in the final version of the play, he does not even get a mention. (16)

For some reason Shakespeare makes certain to praise an earl of Oxford when history makes that possible and to write an earl of Oxford entirely out of history when an accurate dramatic portrayal of the man would bring discredit to the Oxford line.

22. William Shakespeare wrote history plays about Henries IV, V, VI and VIII but not about Henry VII, the founder of the Tudor dynasty. This curious omission helps to bolster the argument for Edward de Vere as having been the author.

According to Oxfordian researcher Robin Fox, Henry VII was a "remark-ably successful" king whose chief policy achievement was to curb the power of the aristocracy and to raise and solidify the power of the middle class.

"He pushed laws through Parliament to restrict the use of liveried retainers —in effect abolishing the private armies the nobles had routinely kept in the past. He let them keep their titles and high-sounding offices ("Lord Great Chamberlain" etc.) but he hemmed them in with taxes and required of them bonds that ruthlessly penalized disloyalty.... He created, in effect, an efficient, central, meritocratic bureaucracy, and in doing so reduced the powers of the aristocracy, which continued to shine at court, but was less likely to usurp royal power." (17)

According to Fox, had Shakespeare actually been the Stratford man, the son of a glover who rose to be a successful poet, playwright, theatre owner and actor, he would likely have been drawn to write a play about Henry VII since Henry did so much to establish and consolidate the power of Shakespeare's putative class. "He was the son of the trading classes aspiring to a coat of arms and the ranks of the gentry. He should have reveled in the memory of Henry VII," wrote Fox. (18)

However, Shakespeare did not write a play about Henry VII. Edward de Vere, the romantic medievalist and champion of the nobility, would have had little sympathy for Henry VII, who established policies that led to the decline of the English aristocracy.

23. De Vere's courtship and marriage with Anne Cecil contain several details that show up in the plays of William Shakespeare.

In winning Anne Cecil, Edward de Vere had to defeat another suitor for her, Philip Sidney, who later became Sir Philip Sidney, the noted poet and soldier. Sir Philip Sidney was the nephew of Robert Dudley, Earl of Leicester, the man who was Elizabeth's special favorite and who probably came closest to being her husband. Personal and financial details of Sidney's courtship of Anne are exactly mirrored in the romantic triangle between Fenton, Slender and Sweet Anne Page in *The Merry Wives of Windsor*.

In 1569, Burghley and Sidney's father agreed that Philip and Anne should marry. They drew up a contract that laid out financial obligations on both sides. The original of this document has been preserved among Burghley's papers, and details from them, when compared with passages from *The Merry Wives*, throw much light on the authorship question.

"The agreement states that on the day of the marriage, Sidney should have an income of £266 a year. As lay rector of Whitford, in Flint, he already had £80 a year; so that, after all charges against the living had been met, his total immediate income would be something over £300 a year." (19)

Now in *The Merry Wives of Windsor*, when the young, marriageable daughter, whose name happens to be Anne, is being pressed by her father and by Slender's friends and his uncle, Robert Shallow, to marry Slender, she expresses her attitude toward the match in the following aside:

> Anne: This is my father's choice. O, what a world
> of vile, ill-favored faults looks handsome
> in three hundred pounds a year.

The marriage contract goes on to stipulate that "at Sidney's father's death, Sidney was to receive an increase of only £147 a year, while at his mother's death he would receive an increase of £325, in all, an increase of £472 a year."

In the play, Slender tells Anne Page,

> I keep but three men and a boy yet, till my mother be dead.
> But what though? Yet I live like a poor gentleman born.

The marriage agreement also offers incentives from the bride's side. It states, "If Anne's younger brother or brethren shall die without issue, Anne Cecil shall have, in reversion, after the death of her father and mother, £200 lands and also a dwelling house within 13 miles of London, meet for a gentleman of £500 lands."

Oxfordian scholar John Thomas Looney writes that this is "an inheritance therefore of exactly £700."

Again, in the play, during Act I, Scene 1, Shallow, Slender and Hugh Evans are discussing how to improve Slender's very slender fortunes. Evans suggests that Slender might marry Anne Page, whom he describes as being a piece of "pretty virginity." He elaborates on her fortune. Shakespeare writes it as if Hugh Evans were speaking in a heavy Welsh accent.

> It is that fery person for all the 'orld,
> as just you well desire, and 700 pounds
> of moneys, and gold and silver,
> is her grandsire upon his death's bed —
> —Got deliver to a joyful resurrections! —
> give, when she is able to overtake
> seventeen years old.

Looney points out that the relationship between William Cecil and his father, Robert Cecil, was very complex and nuanced with various grudges and recriminations which affect the grandfather's will. He says that because of those grudges, the grandfather's modest fortune was directed to devolve only upon Anne and that the will was not clarified or even revealed until the grandfather was in his final sickness and was living at William Cecil's house, confined to bed. Therefore, according to Looney, the line from Hugh Evans' speech, "her grandsire upon his death's bed," fits perfectly and seems to indicate that the author was drawing on his intimate knowledge with one particular family, the family of William Cecil. (20)

Another congruity. The marriage contract states that Anne was to receive a jointure upon marrying Sidney. A jointure is a cash prize, similar to a signing bonus in sports. The marriage agreement does not mention an amount for the jointure, but in the play, the man who represents the character of Leicester, does.

In Act III, Scene 4, Shallow is pressing the proposal of Slender, as he stands sheepishly and stupidly on. Shallow and Anne are talking, and Shallow says,

"He will make you a hundred and fifty pounds jointure." To which Anne replies, "Good Master Shallow, let him woo for himself."

In the actual, real-world courtship between Anne Cecil and Philip Sidney, something apparently went wrong with the Sidney proposal sometime in the year 1570. Instead, William Cecil was elevated to the baronage in February 1571 and Edward de Vere married Anne Cecil in December 1571, a few weeks after Anne had turned fifteen.

24. The marriage to Anne Cecil is also mirrored in *All's Well That Ends Well*, in which Helena, a young woman of non-noble (or "common") blood, falls in love with Bertram, a young nobleman. Helena was raised in the same household as Bertram; for ten years, de Vere lived in the same household as Anne.

25. Recall that after his father's death in 1562, Edward de Vere became a ward of the crown. In *All's Well That Ends Well*, the first few lines of the play tell the same story:

Countess of Rousillon:

In delivering my son from me, I bury a second husband.

Bertram, her son:

And I, in going, madam, weep o'er my father's death anew, but I must attend His Majesty's command, to whom I am now in ward, evermore in subjection.

26. There is a legend about de Vere concerning his unusual relations with Anne Cecil. It was said of him that one time, when he had resolved not to sleep with her, he had made an assignation to have sexual relations with another woman. This agreement was overheard by Burghley's spies, who told Burghley, who was desperate that sexual congress between his daughter and her husband should occur (otherwise after two years the marriage could be annulled.)

Burghley arranged a switch between the other woman and his daughter, so that de Vere unwittingly had sexual congress with Anne after all. (21)

It is notable that this legend hung about de Vere during his life and for four centuries afterward, until the present day. The same episode occurs in *All's Well That Ends Well* and *Measure For Measure*.

27. A rumor about how much money William Shakespeare spent each year exactly corresponds to how much money Edward de Vere received annually from the crown.

Reverend John Ward was vicar of Stratford on Avon from 1662 to 1681. During that time he kept a series of diaries. In the diary for the years 1661 to 1663, Ward wrote down some information that he had gathered about Stratford's most famous son, William Shakespeare. Reverend Ward wrote that Shakespeare "supplied the stage with two plays every year, and for that he had an allowance so large that he spent at the rate of £1000 a year, as I have heard."

Scholars have rejected this information about Shakespeare as being out of the question, far too high for a poet, playwright and theatre-owner to have earned, even one as successful as Shakespeare.

Yet Edward de Vere, as it happens, received an annuity of exactly that amount. It was given to him by express order of Queen Elizabeth, beginning in 1586 and continuing throughout her reign and until his death in June 1604.

28. Many parallels exist between the language and imagery that are used in the Works and those found in the surviving letters, poems and prefaces of de Vere.

Let one example stand for a thousand. It concerns William Shakespeare's use of the Biblical phrase, "I am that I am." In the Bible (Exodus, Chapter 3, Verses 13 and 14) Moses asks the Lord, "When I come to the children of Israel and shall say unto them, The God of your fathers hath sent me unto you: and they shall say to me, What is his name? What shall I say unto them?

And God said unto Moses, I AM THAT I AM."

William Shakespeare uses that same phrase in Sonnet 121.

> T'is better to be vile than vile esteemed
> When not to be receives reproach of being,
> And the just pleasure lost, which is so deemed
> Not by our feeling, but by others' seeming.
> For why should others' false adulterate eyes
> Give salutation to my sportive blood?
> Or on my frailties why are frailer spies
> Which in their wills count bad what I think good?
> No, I am that I am, and they that level
> At my abuses reckon up their own;
> I may be straight though they themselves be bevel,
> By their rank thoughts my deeds must not be shown.
> Unless this general evil they maintain:
> All men are bad and in their badness reign.

Very few men quote God at any time, but even fewer will talk about themselves in the same words that God has used to talk about Himself. Especially in a time when faith in God and the fear of God were strong, it is quite rare, it is almost unique, because it implies that the writer equates himself with God.

Edward de Vere used the same phrase in a letter he wrote to William Burghley in 1584. Burghley had been using de Vere's servants to spy on him, and de Vere wrote him a note to ask him to stop the vile practice. "I serve Her Majesty, and I am that I am, and by alliance near your Lordship, but free, and scorn to be offered that injury to think that I am so weak of government as to be ruled by servants, and not able to govern myself."

So Edward de Vere and William Shakespeare both used a well-known Biblical phrase, but they used it in a rare way—not in connection with religious or devotional matters, but in a secular context. In each instance, they used it to defend themselves.

Other parallels abound and are too numerous to detail here. The reader is referred to *Shakespeare Identified* by J.T. Looney, *Alias Shakespeare* by Joseph Sobran and *Shakespeare Revealed In Oxford's Letters* by William Plumer Fowler.

29. Attributing the authorship to Edward de Vere eases the chronological concerns that seem insuperable if authorship is attributed to William Shakspere of Stratford.

    If we accept the Stratford man as the author, we must accept that he wrote the sonnets to a man he did not know (22), as a father to a son, and from the point of view of a middle aged man, while he himself was still a relatively young man. (William Shakspere was 26 years old in 1590.) We must accept that he wrote uproarious and exuberant comedies at the same time that he was writing gloomy and despairing sonnets, and when the mood of the country was dark and unsettled.

    Also, we must accept that he had a long period of intellectual and creative decline, in which he wrote plays that exhibited far less polish and sophistication than did his great masterpieces.

    However, if one would insist in attributing authorship to the Stratford man, none of these reservations is impossible to overcome. Some scholars have attempted to explain the baffling mystery of the sonnets by asserting that they were written as literary exercises and have nothing to do with the poet's actual life.

    However, when Edward de Vere is credited with authorship many (but not all) of these problems disappear. The dates of Shakespeare's career are moved back to the period from 1574 to 1604. Within this time frame, the early comedies with their high spirits and polished courtly wit seem to fit more naturally in the first decade of writing than they do if they are placed in the 1588-1594 time period, when Elizabeth was approaching sixty years old, when several attempts were made upon her life and when a possible war of succession loomed.

Under the Oxfordian theory of authorship, the "dotage" plays—*Timon of Athens, Cymbeline, Pericles* and others—can now be placed early in the Bard's career and be seen as apprentice pieces.

The Oxfordian interpretation allows us to credit Shakespeare with originality as well as genius. He did not imitate and refine Lyly, Kyd and Marlowe; he was their exemplar.

However, under the de Vere hypothesis, it is necessary to accept that the author revised his plays during the last fourteen years of his life.

As for the argument that Oxford's death in 1604 would have precluded him from writing *The Tempest, Othello, King Lear, Antony and Cleopatra, The Winter's Tale* and the other so-called late plays, that problem has been dealt with by several Oxfordian scholars. Roger Stritmatter and Lynn Kositsky have demonstrated that the 1611 date for *The Tempest* is unwarranted (23). Charles Wisner Barrell demonstrated back in the 1940s that the late play *The Winter's Tale* was likely first performed in 1593. (24) Richard Whalen examines the dating of twelve so-called "late" plays and gives credible reasons for eliminating certainty for lateness from all twelve. (25) For as orthodox Shakespearean scholar E. K. Chambers has written, "There is much of conjecture, even as regards the order, and still more as regards the ascriptions to particular years ... These (plays) are partly arranged to provide a fairly smooth even flow of production when plague and other interruptions did not inhibit it." (26)

In other words, even the greatest of orthodox Shakespearean scholars admits that the exact dates for the plays are a matter of conjecture. It is clear that much orthodox scholarly certitude is based on the necessity of fitting 37 plays into the 23 years between 1588 and 1611; fitting them into the 30 years offered by Oxford's creative period is, in some important respects, more reasonable and more credible.

30. Episodes and characters from de Vere's life show up in the plays. On May 20, 1573, two of Burghley's servants, Mr. Faunt and Mr. Wotton, were waylaid on the road near Gad's Hill, some 25 miles east of London. The assailants were servants of the Earl of Oxford. Similar episodes, also situated at Gad's Hill, figure prominently in *The Famous Victories of Henry V* and in *Henry IV, Part One*.

31. A detail from Edward de Vere's life suggests a minor detail in *Hamlet*.

    In August 1579 Oxford wanted to play tennis on a court that was then occupied by Philip Sidney, the noted poet and soldier of the Elizabethan era. Oxford ordered him off the court, Sidney refused to leave; the two nearly came to blows, and Sidney finally left. Sidney later challenged Oxford to a duel; Oxford ignored the challenge.

    Sidney was later criticized by the Queen for the episode. She reminded him that when gentry fail to show respect to nobility, then nobility will fail to show respect to royalty, and the people as a whole will fail to show respect to the law and to the country, and anarchy will ensue.

    In *Hamlet* (II, 1, line 59), Polonius tutors a servant on how to draw out evidence from a third person that might be used against Laertes, Polonius's son, to find out how he has been living in Paris. While roaming freely over the subject, Polonius fantasizes that, after being properly primed, a person might be tempted to divulge Laertes' failings. One of the failings that Polonius hypothetically mentions is "falling out at tennis."

32. Another detail from de Vere's life explains Hamlet's otherwise obscure remark about being "but mad north-northwest."

    Martin Frobisher was an English navigator and explorer who made three trips to North America, in 1576, 1577 and 1578. He was seeking the Northwest Passage to China and India. De Vere invested £3000 ($1 million) in the 1578 voyage, the commercial object of which was to bring back 1200 tons of supposedly gold-laced ore from Canada—Meta Incognita—and to make the investors rich beyond measure.

    The trip was a bust; the dirt contained fool's gold, and de Vere's diminishing estates became more diminished. Other trips to find the Northwest Passage occurred in 1584 and 1585. De Vere also invested in them, but in lesser amounts.

    Hamlet says, "I am but mad north-northwest." (II, 2, 387)

33. The name of the agent who arranged the financial backing for the 1578 voyage of Martin Frobisher—the one that de Vere invested and lost £3000 in—was Michael Lok. In *The Merchant of Venice*, the name of the Jew is Shylock.

34. Also, in *The Merchant of Venice*, what is the amount of the bond that Antonio writes to Shylock? 3000 ducats.

35. The character of Fluellen in *Henry V* has been thought to be modeled on that of soldier of fortune and military author Roger Williams. This idea has been offered to the scholarly public by Stratfordians Sir Henry Lee and Professor

John Dover Wilson, who came to that conclusion separately. Oxfordian researcher Charles Wisner Barrell discovered that Roger Williams was a retainer of the Earl of Oxford. (27)

36. In *The Merry Wives of Windsor*, the character of Hugh Evans seems to be a caricature of Henry Evans, a man who was a close associate of the Earl of Oxford's.

In the play, Sir Hugh Evans is a Welshman who observes the action throughout, acts as a friend to Shallow and Slender, and, in the final act, directs a group of children and adults to dance as faeries in the wood, in order to terrorize and comically torment the butt of the play, Sir John Falstaff.

In Oxford's life, there is a figure who closely resembles Hugh Evans. This is Henry Evans, a Welshman who was the manager of the Children of St. Paul's theatrical troupe. Here is Oxfordian scholar Robert Brazil talking about Henry Evans:

"He started out as a scrivener and theatrical hanger-on. In the years 1584 to 1586, the Earl of Oxford arranged to lease a large hall in the liberty of Blackfriars for use as a playhouse, subletting the downstairs to the fencing master, Rocco Bonetti, for his fencing school. A complicated paper trail on this still exists, showing payments that connect Oxford as patron, John Lyly as go-between and proprietor, and Henry Evans as theatre manager. Their troupe of young actors was created by combining the Children of Paul's with the Children of the Chapel, the combined group sometimes referred to "Oxford's Boys." They were not just making random entertainments; throughout the 1580s, they performed regularly for the Queen and her Court and for private audiences." (28)

37. The Vavasor affair brought retribution against de Vere from Vavasor's family members and their clan. These attacks may have resulted in de Vere's becoming lame. William Shakespeare in the sonnets twice admits to being lame.

In the late 1570s, Edward de Vere had an affair with Anne Vavasor, a beautiful and vivacious Gentlewoman of the Queen's Bedchamber. In March, 1581, Vavasor gave birth to a son, whom she named Edward Vere. A day after giving birth, Vavasor and son were confined in the Tower. Edward de Vere was also confined in the Tower soon after, and was kept there from April until June, 1581. De Vere was banished from court for two years as punishment for his affair with Vavasor.

A year after Anne Vavasor gave birth, her uncle, Thomas Knyvet, began a feud with de Vere. De Vere and his employees engaged in a series of three street fights with Knyvet and his men. In one fight de Vere was badly injured.

A court observer notes in a letter that "both men were injured, but the Earl of Oxford the more dangerously."

Years later, de Vere mentioned in various letters that he had become lame.

"Wherefore when your Lordship shall have best time and leisure, if I may know it I will attend your lordship as well as a lame man might in your house."—a letter to Burghley, March 1595.

"I am sorry that I have not an able body which might have served to attend on Her Majesty."—letter to Burghley, Sept. 1597.

In his sonnets, William Shakespeare twice mentions his lameness: "So I, made lame by Fortune's dearest spite" (Sonnet 37) and "Speak of my lameness, and straight I will halt." (Sonnet 89.)

So both Shakespeare and de Vere were lame.

38. The three violent clashes between the gangs of de Vere and Knyvet suggest the number of clashes between the Montagues and the Capulets in *Romeo and Juliet*. Note the Prince of Verona's speech at the beginning of the play:

> Three civil brawls bred of an airy word
> by thee, old Capulet and Montague,
> have thrice disturbed the quiet of our streets....

> *Romeo and Juliet*, Act I, Scene 1

39. These clashes in the wake of the Vavasor affair find an echo in *Hamlet*.

Recall that in the play, Hamlet inadvertently intercepts a letter from Claudius in which Claudius arranges for Hamlet's murder. (V, 2, 12-24)

According to Elizabeth Sears, Thomas Knyvet's 1582 attack on Oxford was of the same character as Claudius's planned murder of Hamlet, that is, it was an attempt at a calculated political murder, an assassination. Sears notes that the clash between Knyvet and Oxford occurred a year after Anne Vavasor had given birth to Oxford's son. She reasons that, therefore, the violence was not motivated by unbridled anger. It was likely a "hit" authorized by Queen Elizabeth herself.

Sears notes that Elizabeth had made Knyvet Keeper of Westminster Palace in January 1582, a month before he attacked Oxford. (29)

40. Another passage from *Romeo and Juliet* points to a connection with the Earl of Oxford. The connection is to Rocco Bonetti, who some scholars suggest was the model for Tybalt.

The Earl of Oxford leased a theatre space in Blackfriars in 1584, and promptly gave the lease to his secretary, John Lyly. Along with the playhouse in the lease was a room on the floor below, which Lyly rented to Italian fencing master Rocco Bonetti, who used the room to host a school of fencing.

George Silver, writing in 1599, wrote that Bonetti was such a fine swordsman that "he would have hit any English man with a thrust, just upon any button in his doublet." (30)

In *Romeo and Juliet*, Shakespeare has Mercutio describe Tybalt in the following way. "He fights as you sing pricksong—keeps time, distance and proportion; rests me his minim rest, one, two, and the third in your bosom! The very butcher of a silk button, a duelist, a duelist! A gentleman of the very first house, of the first and second cause. Ah, the immortal passado! The punto reverso! The hay!"

Later in the same passage, Mercutio utters words that make the connection to Bonetti crystal clear.

"Why, is this not a lamentable thing, grand sir, that we should be thus afflicted with these strange flies. These fashion mongers, these pardona mees, who stand so much on the new form that they cannot sit at ease on the old bench? O, their bones, their bones!" (*Romeo and Juliet*, II, 4, 20-36)

So, assuming that Oxford visited Blackfriars while his secretary was running it as a theatre, and assuming that while there, on occasion, he also visited the fencing school on the floor below, we once again see that a person from the life of the Earl of Oxford can be recognized as a character in a Shakespeare play.

41. Markings and personal notations found in de Vere's copy of the Bible suggest that it was, literally, the very copy that William Shakespeare used.

    In 1570, Edward de Vere purchased a copy of the Geneva Bible. (The bible is now in the possession of the Folger Shakespeare Library in Washington, D.C.). He underscored or otherwise emphasized more than a thousand passages—1,028 passages to be exact—in this bible.

    In 1990, Roger Stritmatter, then a Ph.D. candidate at University of Massachusetts, Amherst, wrote a dissertation on these marginalia. He determined that of the 1028 marginalia or emphasized passages, approximately 250 occur in recognizable form in the plays.

42. Evidence is strong both that William Shakespeare wrote the play *Sir Thomas More*, and that Edward de Vere wrote the play as William Shakespeare.

Sir Thomas More is an anonymously written Elizabethan play that was discovered in manuscript form as part of the Harleian Manuscripts, which were sold to the British Library in 1753.

The manuscripts were part of the collection of Sir Robert Harley, First Earl of Oxford (of the second creation), and his son, Edward Harley, the Second Earl. They were likely sold to the British Library by the Second Earl's widow, Lady Henrietta Cavendish Holles Harley, who had ancestry back to the original Vere family. (31) The play was first published in 1844.

It is a remarkable and controversial play for many reasons. The manuscript is apparently incomplete. It consists of the main body of the play and is accompanied by several additions, short scenes that were appended in a group to the play. These additions were all written in different "hands" or handwriting, leading several scholars to conclude that composition of the play was either a collaborative effort, or was dictated by a single author to many different secretaries. The manuscript also bears written comments from Elizabeth's censor, who criticized various scenes of the play and who ordered deletions and other changes. Because of the severity of his comments, it is thought that the play was never performed.

Most importantly, from about 1871 various scholars have thought that at least one scene, the so-called "Hand D" scene in which Sir Thomas More quells a riot by his eloquent appeal to the mob that it bow to the logic of Elizabethan social hierarchy, was written by William Shakespeare. (32)

More recently, some scholars have found in *Sir Thomas More* numerous parallels to passages in Shakespeare. Fran Gridley, writing in *The Oxfordian* (2003), notes fifteen cases in which lines from Sir Thomas More mirror or strongly echo lines from various Shakespeare plays, including the instance when the character Doll Williamson echoes one of Shakespeare's most famous lines, when she says, "I do owe God a death, and I must pay him" which is close to the line "A man can die but once, we owe God a death," from *2 Henry IV*. (33)

Gridley finds that the author of *Sir Thomas More* uses humor in a similar way and manipulates time in the same way as Shakespeare, compressing it or expanding it as he feels necessary.

Gridley also finds parallels between the Hand D scene mentioned above and Mark Antony's funeral oration from *Julius Caesar*. The parallels are:

1) that in *Julius Caesar*, Antony begins, "Friends, Romans, countrymen...." and in *More*, Sir Thomas begins, "Friends, masters, countrymen..." and

2) that after Mark Antony's speech, the inflamed citizenry cry, "Fire the houses!", while in *More*, before the speech, the citizens cry, "Fire the houses!"

Moreover, some researchers are now using computers to compare linguistic style to assess authorship. One such is Thomas Merriam, who used a computer to analyze *Sir Thomas More* and three other canonical plays of Shakespeare against a standard which he called a composite value for Shakespeare.

Doing this yielded a .45 for *Julius Caesar*, .40 for *King Lear*, .35 for *Pericles* and a .26 for *Sir Thomas More*. To put these findings in perspective, using the same computer program to analyze Anthony Munday's *John a Kent and John a Cumber* as a possible Shakespeare play yielded a value of .000000163. (34)

Accepting that the play is Shakespeare's, how can we prove that the play is de Vere's? First, two allusions in the play indicate that it was written circa 1580, when the Stratford man was a boy of sixteen. One allusion refers to a minor religious movement that was active in England between 1579 and 1582, that of Robert Brown, who claimed to be a cousin of Lord Burghley. Brown advocated for vigorous churches that were not under the control either of the state or of church establishment; he was arrested 32 times between 1579 and 1582. Brownists affected simplicity of dress and wore their hair short.

In *Sir Thomas More*, Faulkner, one of the characters, after receiving a haircut, says that he looks "thus like a Brownist." Since Robert Brown was sent into exile in 1582, his influence would have waned soon after that year. Therefore, *Sir Thomas More* can be dated to 1579 to 1584.

Another chronological clue in *Sir Thomas More* occurs in Scene 9, when one of the actors has to "run to Oagles for a beard." Shakespearean scholar Walter W. Greg notes that "a John Oagle or Owgle appears in this capacity (of wig-maker) in the Revels' Accounts for 1572-3 and 1584-5." Gridley concludes that "surely the dramatist named a real wigmaker from his own time." (35)

The most weighty of reasons for attributing authorship to Edward de Vere is that the body of play is written in the handwriting of Anthony Munday, who was de Vere's secretary from 1579 to 1581 or 1582. It is clear that the Protestant Munday would not have written a hagiographic play about the Catholic More; however, de Vere was a Catholic between 1576 and 1582 and so More's Catholicism would not have prevented de Vere from lionizing him.

Finally, the author of *Sir Thomas More* not only used Roper's *Life of More* as a source for the play, but he used a manuscript version of the book. This manuscript version could not have been available to William Shakspere, who was a boy in Stratford during the time of the play's composition, but it could have been available to Edward de Vere.

As Charles F. Herberger writes, "If the play was written in 1580, as seems likely, Shakspere of Stratford was a sixteen year old boy living in a provincial town. His access to books of any kind would have been severely limited, to say nothing of rare manuscripts.

"On the other hand, Anthony Munday was a friend and close associate of the historian John Stowe, who collected rare manuscripts as sources for his chronicle .... To see Stowe as the provider of Munday with rare manuscripts for Oxford's use is a very plausible link. It would explain how a manuscript of Roper's *More* came into Oxford's hands as a source of an early play that was not allowed to be performed because it portrayed More—the Catholic martyr executed by Henry VIII—in a favorable light." (36)

43. The fact that Martin Droeshout used a painting of Jacobean poet Sir Thomas Overbury as a model for Shakespeare for the cover for the book *Mr. William Shakespeare's Comedies, Histories and Tragedies* (otherwise known as the First Folio, 1623) proves that William Shakespeare, "the Swan of Avon", was a fiction and a cover-up for the real author.

In 2009, the Anglo-Irish art collector and musicologist Sir Alec Cobbe announced to the world the he had found a previously unknown contemporary portrait of William Shakespeare. The announcement drew headlines, with articles on the Cobbe Portrait of Shakespeare appearing in *Time*, *Newsweek* and newspapers around the world. However, almost immediately the announcement brought a counter-current of dissent.

The Stratfordian scholar Katharine Duncan-Jones quickly concluded that the portrait was not of Shakespeare, but was of the obscure Jacobean poet Sir Thomas Overbury. And indeed, when one compares the Cobbe Portrait with other pictures of Overbury, their identity is total. Also a glance at both the Cobbe Portrait and the Droeshout engraving of Shakespeare presents a stunning parallel: the same arched eyebrows, straight Grecian nose, the same rounded pouches under the eyes, the same feminine mouth. It is fascinating to observe how the insolence of Overbury in the Cobbe Portrait becomes, in the Droeshout engraving, the idiocy of Shakespeare.

Sir Thomas Overbury was a friend, secretary and mentor of Robert Carr, who was himself the favorite of the bisexual king, James I. As Carr rose in James' esteem, so did the influence and power of Overbury grow. It was said of him, "Overbury governed Carr and Carr governed the King." James eventually made Carr the Earl of Rochester. (37)

Carr became romantically involved with Frances Howard, Countess of Essex, a married woman. When Overbury understood that a marriage between Rochester and Howard would curb his influence, he opposed the marriage, and bluntly told Carr of the Countess's failings. The Lady Essex, who had by this time become Countess of Rochester, conspired with James to have Overbury imprisoned and then to have Tower servants slowly poison him. Overbury died of poisoning in November 1613 while imprisoned in the Tower.

The truth came out in the trial that followed, reflecting badly not only upon Frances Howard, but also upon the Earl of Rochester and King James. It reflected well upon Overbury, however, and sales of his books shot up. Whereas in life he had been a minor poet and prose stylist, in death, he became a champion.

By 1622, James had a new favorite, the Duke of Buckingham, and a marriageable son, Prince Charles. James and Buckingham sought to marry Charles to the Spanish Infanta, a move that was seen by many as a catastrophe in the making. The Spanish marriage, on the eve of publication of the First Folio, was the hottest political question in England. The marriage was vigorously opposed by both Henry Wriothesley, the Third Earl of Southampton, and by Henry de Vere, the 18th Earl of Oxford.

In 1623, when the earls of Pembroke and Montgomery, the two noble brethren who were the financial backers of the First Folio, came to publish the book, they needed an image to represent the fictional author, William Shakespeare. They could not use a picture of Edward de Vere, for they had decided to keep the true identity of the author hidden. They directed Droeshout to base his 'artist's impression of Shakespeare' on Overbury, both to suggest that the contents of the book were "true English" i.e., not of the weak and corrupt party of James, and that the true identity of the real author had been, as it were, *buried over*.

Droeshout complied, and gave to the world that image of William Shakespeare of which the painter Thomas Gainsborough once said that he had never seen a stupider face. (38) Those who may wish to see the Cobbe portrait, and to verify for themselves that it really is of Sir Thomas Overbury, may find images of it online.

Go to Mark Anderson's Oxfordian website, shakespearebyanothername.com, then go to the blogspot, then to the year 2009, then to March, when most of Anderson's fine articles on the question were written.

44. Edward de Vere used two common words, ever and never, to signify himself and to assert his authorship when he was forbidden to do so by the Queen and her counselors.

From his youth on, de Vere was compelled to write anonymously. He translated Ovid's *Metamorphoses* while still a teenager and published it under the name of his uncle, Arthur Golding. He wrote numerous lyrics that bejewel the plays of his secretary, John Lyly, which have been assumed for centuries to have been Lyly's.

He wrote several poems that were published in collections such as *England's Helicon* (1600 and 1614) over the name Ignoto, a pseudonym that suggests Unknown, Ignotus. And also, he wrote the plays and poems of William Shakespeare under that famous alias.

Throughout this enforced anonymity, de Vere left various verbal clues to his identity. Unfortunately, two of the most often used clues happen to be the extremely common words 'ever" and "never." To the skeptic, the author's use of such words prove nothing; but to the initiated (if I may use that word) these words are the anonymous author's secret signature hidden in plain sight.

Ever is a compression of E.Ver(e) for Edward de Vere. Never is its opposite. It implies that the great poet was identifying with his own negation, or, put another way, that he was equally asserting his identity as an eternally living poet and as a total failure whose name would never be remembered.

Understanding that the author used these common words in this arcane way adds another level of meaning to some of Shakespeare's texts; in some instances, it provides the only way to render the line or sentence intelligible.

For example, it helps to explain the second quatrain of Sonnet 76.

> Why write I still all one, ever the same,
> And keep invention in a noted weed,
> That every word doth almost tell my name,
> Showing their birth, and where they did proceed?

If we think that the author of the Works was William Shakspere, the man from Stratford, it is difficult to make sense of the third line in the quatrain quoted above. In what sense does every word tell the name Shakespeare? Is he saying that his writing style and his theme are so monotonous that no one else sounds like him? To an extent, yes. But he's saying more than that. He's saying that "every word doth almost tell my name." We want to take the line literally, but, if we accept that the author's name was Will, or William, or Shakespeare, or William Shakespeare, the line makes no sense. But when we understand that de Vere is the author, then we see that the line is a very deft pun:

> "That every word doth almost tell my name"

Here are a few more examples of how de Vere used the words ever and never to encrypt his name.

From *All's Well That Ends Well* (Act V, 3) from Bertram's final speech in the play.

> If she, my liege, can make me know this clearly,
> I'll love her dearly, ever, ever dearly.

The repetition of "ever' seems vacuous, a rare trait in Shakespeare's writing. Also we may note that the "ever, ever" are surrounded in the sentence by "dearly" and "dearly": more vacuity, until we recognize that the word "earl" is concealed in "dearly." So either the line is the apotheosis of vacuity, a line which Colley Cibber might have written and crossed out, or, it is a quadrupal signature: the earl, E. Vere; E. Vere, the earl.

In *Antony and Cleopatra* (V,2), after Antony has died and Cleopatra is contemplating suicide, a clown enters bearing the asp. In 32 lines, the word "worm" is mentioned nine times, eight by the clown and once by Cleopatra.

The clown mentions it in odd ways. He says, "the worm's an odd worm," "I wish you all joy of the worm," and "Yes, forsooth, I wish you joy o' th' worm."

Worm in French is "ver." The repetition of it is the author's autograph in a foreign language.

One of Shakespeare's most famous sonnets is replete with examples of this usage. In order to see the encrypted signature, you must first understand that one of de Vere's family insignia was the mullet, the five pointed star. Now, re-read these lines from Sonnet 116:

> O no, it is an ever-fixed mark,
> That looks on tempests and is never shaken.
> It is the star to every wandering bark,
> Whose worth's unknown, although his height be taken.

Here we see that love has become a talisman, almost a god. The author says it will never perish and never change. But if we credit the theory that de Vere was Shakespeare, we see that the poet is saying that love is synonymous with the author himself, that love is an "ever-fixed mark" which is "the star to every wandering bark."

We might also note that the author signed himself twice in the sonnet's final line:

> If this be error, and upon me proved,
> I never writ, nor no man ever loved.

We see this usage most pointedly in the preface to the 1609 quarto edition of *Troilus and Cressida*. This preface praises the work of Shakespeare and claims that *Troilus and Cressida* has never been performed publicly.
Here is how it begins:

> A never writer, to an ever reader: newes.

> Eternal reader, you have here a new play, never staled with the stage, never clapper-clawed with the palms of the vulgar...

Although I have chosen not to relate the preface in full and not to explore all of its implications, the use of "ever" and "never" in the first line is curious. Taken at face value, the line makes no sense. For how can a writer be a "never writer"? And why would a reader of a Shakespeare play be styled an "ever reader"?

But if we recognize that ever and never are codes for E. Vere, Edward de Vere, the title line makes sense and the author is identified.

Finally from *King Lear*, in the greatest scene in all drama (V. 3), after Lear has carried in the dead Cordelia and is raving in his agony:

> And my poor fool is hang'd? No, no, no life?
> Why should a dog, a horse, a rat have life
> And thou no breath at all? Thou'lt come no more,
> Never, never, never, never, never.

Here the possibilities for conjecture become almost infinite.

Some authors have gone very far afield in this line of inquiry. (39) They've asserted that Shakespeare, like James Joyce, used words from multiple languages to make puns, but that, unlike Joyce, Shakespeare used them to leave clues pointing to his true identity. Such authors may be correct; I do not know. What I am asserting here is that, on occasion, Shakespeare uses the words "ever" and "never" to signify himself. This formula is key to solving one of the most intractable of Shakespearean riddles, the dedication to *Shakespeare's Sonnets*.

45. One interpretation to the mysterious dedication to *Shakespeare's Sonnets* yields a message that they were all written by Edward de Vere.

The dedication to the sonnets has long baffled and titillated scholars and readers alike. It is perhaps the oddest dedication in all of English literature, the more so because it is the dedication to one of the greatest classics of our literature and it appears to make next to no sense.

Here is the dedication as it appears in the 1609 edition of *Shakespeare's Sonnets*.

TO.THE.ONLIE.BEGETTER.OF.
THESE.INSUING.SONNETS.
M^r. W. H. ALL.HAPPINESSE.
AND.THAT.ETERNITIE.
PROMISED.
BY.

OUR.EVER-LIVING.POET.
WISHETH.

THE.WELL-WISHING.
ADVENTURER.IN.
SETTING.
FORTH.

T.T.

In 1997, the English mathematician and scholar John Rollett published an essay in which he offered a solution to the riddle of the dedication. Taking for granted that Edward de Vere often used the common words ever and never to represent or signify himself, as in ever=E.Vere=Edward de Vere, and recognizing that the period after each of the words in the dedication presumably means something, Rollett observed that the dedication is physically structured in three inverted pyramids and that there are six lines in the first pyramid, two lines in the second and four lines in the third pyramid.

He further noted that Edward de Vere has six letters in his first name, two in his middle name (the "de") and four in his last name, Vere. He then guessed that the periods after each word in the dedication indicated that the reader is to count the words and that the triple-pyramidal structure of the dedication means that the reader is to count every sixth, second, and fourth, word.

Rollett found that doing so yields the message "These sonnets all by ever."

He continued to investigate the dedication, arranging the letters into various cryptographic arrays. A cryptographic array is a simple decoding device in which a text is placed in a grid pattern with punctuation excluded. The grid can be of any length, so long as each line is the same length (except for the last line, which will vary as the number of letters vary.) Using such arrays, hidden messages can then become apparent in the vertical, horizontal or diagonal directions.

Rollet found that when the dedication to the sonnets was arranged in a fifteen-letter array, the word "Henry" is spelled vertically. He also found that when the dedication was arranged into an eighteen-letter array, the very uncommon name "Wriothesley" can be found in three sections. Rollet calculated that the odds of this happening by chance are one in 30 billion. (40)

46. Even when taken at face value, the dedication to the sonnets implies that the author was dead by the date of publication.

   If (as is reasonable to suppose) the phrase "our ever-living poet" refers to the author of the sonnets, then he was dead in 1609, which was the year they were first published. This is because "ever-living" means "he will live forever"; it is spoken of someone who has recently died and of course refers to his legacy, his importance, his legend or the memory that people who will be alive in the future will bear toward him, the deceased. Edward de Vere died in 1604; William Shakspere died in 1616.

   The dedication of the sonnets tells us that the author could not have been William Shakspere, the actor from Stratford.

47. The Ashbourne Portrait, which was discovered in 1847 and given to the world as a portrait of William Shakespeare, has now been proven to be a portrait of the Earl of Oxford.

Dutch painter Cornelus Ketel visited England from 1573 to 1581. He is recorded as having painted a portrait of the Earl of Oxford, which subsequently became lost.

In March, 1847 an English schoolmaster named Clement Usill Kingston claimed to have found an original contemporary painting of William Shakespeare. The subject of the painting did not look like the subject in either the Droeshout engraving or the Chandos Portrait, the two most widely accepted images of the poet, which, however, do not resemble each other. Nevertheless, various art experts inspected the painting and declared it to be of Shakespeare, and in the mid to late 19th Century it was mentioned in at least two books of paintings of Shakespeare.

In 1937, Oxfordian writer Charles Wisner Barrell examined the painting with X-ray and infra-red photography, and determined that the portrait had been altered. The notation "Aetatis Suae 47 A?.1611" had been added in different paint from other gold work in the painting, the family heraldic device had been painted over, and the (presumably) full head of hair of the subject had been painted out and replaced with an oversized bald pate.

Barrell discovered that the portrait had formerly been the property of the Stafford family, an English noble family. It was once the possession of Countess Henrietta Maria Stanley, Countess of Stafford and the great granddaughter of Edward de Vere. A 1695 will of the Earl of Stafford mentions that the family possessed a full length portrait of the Earl of Oxford. In 1721, the art critic and historian George Vertue mentioned that the family was in possession of Ketel's Oxford portrait. But by 1782, the family no longer had the Oxford portrait. Instead, they now had a three-quarter length portrait of William Shakespeare.

A close comparison of the face in the portrait shows it to be identical to the 1575 Welbeck portrait of the Earl of Oxford. As Mark Anderson did in his 2005 book, *Shakespeare By Another Name*, when the paintings are halved, and the halves placed next to each other, they make a full portrait of Edward de Vere, who as late as the mid-18th Century, was recognized by his descendants as having been the real William Shakespeare.

It has often been asked, how does the fact that the Ashbourne Portrait is a painting of Edward de Vere prove that he was Shakespeare?

It does in this way. We must remember that the Ashbourne Portrait was presented to the world in 1847 as a portrait of William Shakespeare. Now, only one of two conditions can be the case in this instance. One possibility is that Reverend Clement Usill Kingston was guessing that the subject was William Shakespeare, and he happened to pick, by accident, the man who would turn out to be the leading candidate for having been the real author.

The chances of his doing that would have been roughly one in a hundred million. (41)

The other possibility is that he was told the true identity of the subject of the painting when he bought it. The odds suggest that the later condition was the case, and that, therefore, Edward de Vere was William Shakespeare.

48. Edward de Vere knew Henry Wriothesley, the Third Earl of Southampton. In fact, Southampton was for several years being pressured to marry de Vere's daughter, Elizabeth Vere.

About 1590, Lord Burghley began to push for a marriage between Henry Wriothesley, Third Earl of Southampton, and Elizabeth Vere, the daughter of Edward de Vere and Anne Cecil, and, therefore, Burghley's granddaughter. As Master of Wards for England, Burghley had the power to arrange and contract marriages for his wards. The wards had a strong motive to accept the arranged marriage; if they declined, they were liable to pay enormous fines to the Master of Wards.

Once we accept that Edward de Vere wrote the works of William Shakespeare, the mystery of the sonnets begins to evaporate. What we now know as the first seventeen of the sonnets, the marriage sonnets or the dynastic sonnets as they are called, were written by a supremely talented older poet to a young man who was contemplating marriage with the poet's daughter. In July 1590, de Vere was 42 years old; Southampton was 16; Elizabeth Vere was 14 or 15.

Although the relationship between Edward de Vere and Henry Wriothesley was very complex (as will be explained in the next essay) this much is clear: unlike William Shakspere of Stratford, Edward de Vere actually knew Henry Wriothesley, the Third Earl of Southampton. He nearly became Southampton's father-in-law.

NOTES

1. Looney, J.T. *Shakespeare Identified in Edward de Vere, Seventeenth Earl of Oxford*, 1975 edition, Vol. I, pgs. 286-290.

2. Sobran, Joseph. *Alias Shakespeare*, pg. 142.

3. For number of sales see Ward, B. M. *The Seventeenth Earl of Oxford*, (1928), pg. 353; for total number of lands in possession of his father, 16th Earl of Oxford, at the time of his death, see the 1562 will of John de Vere in Oxdocs at www.socrates.berkeley.edu/ahnelson/

4. Green, Nina. "An Earl in Bondage," *The Shakespeare Oxford Newsletter, Vol. 40*, (No. 3, Summer 2004), pg. 13.

5. Schoenbaum. Samuel. *Shakespeare's Lives*, 1970, pg. 40.

6. Saunders, Sam. "Arthur Goldings's First Decade of Translation: A Brief Examination" *The Shakespeare Oxford Newsletter, Vol. 41* (No. 3, Summer 2005).

7. Altrocchi, Paul. "Edward de Vere as Translator of Ovid's Metamorphoses" *The Shakespeare Oxford Newsletter, Vol. 41*, (No. 2, Spring 2005).

8. Miller, J. Valcour, "Corambis, Polonius and the Great Lord Burghley in Hamlet", in Miller, Ruth Loyd, *Oxfordian Vistas*, page 432. *Oxfordian Vistas* is Volume II of R.L. Miller's 1975 edition of *Shakespeare Identified* by John Thomas Looney. J. Valcour Miller's essay collects numerous observations and conclusions on the question of the real-life original of Polonius which have been published since 1869.

9. This surprisingly intimate factoid comes from the Earl of Oxford himself. Lord Burghley noted in his diary record of a conversation that he had had with Henry Howard, a backfriend of de Vere's, concerning the paternity of Elizabeth Vere: "He confessed to my Lord Howard that he lay not with his wife but at Hampton Court, and that the child could not be his because the child was born in July which was not the space of twelve months." In Philips, G. W., *Lord Burghley in Shakespeare*, pgs. 102 and 103.

10. Anderson, Mark. *Shakespeare By Another Name*, pg. 191.

11. *Encyclopedia Britannica*, 1966 edition. Entries for Vere, Sir Francis, and Vere, Horace. For burial in Westminster Abbey, see Looney, J.T., *Shakespeare Identified in Edward de Vere, the Seventeenth Earl of Oxford*, Miller edition, 1975, Volume 1, page 535.

12. Hannas, Andrew. "Beowulf, Hamlet and Edward de Vere." *The Shakespeare Oxford Newsletter, Volume 26* (No. 2, Spring 1990).

13. Looney, J.T. *Shakespeare identified as Edward de Vere, the Seventeenth Earl of Oxford*, 1975 edition, Volume 1, pgs. 186 and 187

14. *Ibid.*

15. *Encyclopedia Britannica*, 1966 edition, entry for Oxford, Robert de Vere

16. Looney, op. cit., pg.183

17. Fox, Robin. "Why Is There No History of Henry VII?" *The Shakespeare Oxford Newsletter,* Volume 46, Number 2, August 2010, pgs. 2 and 3

18. *Ibid.*

19. Looney, J.T. "The Earl of Oxford as Shakespeare," quoted in "Looney, J.T., *Shakespeare Identified as Edward de Vere, Seventeenth Earl of Oxford, Volume 2* (*Oxfordian Vistas*), edited by Ruth Loyd Miller, page 168 and following

20. *Ibid.*, pg. 174

21. Wright, Thomas. *History and Topography of the County of Essex* (1836).

22. Ogburn, Dorothy and Charlton. *This Star of England*, pg. 1241. The crucial quotation is, "Mrs. C.C. Stopes confessed that, in writing her biography of the Third Earl of Southampton, she spent eight years of industrious and painstaking research, ransacking the public records office, in the hope of finding some connection between Southampton and "Shakespeare" but found absolutely nothing; in consequence she felt that her life had been a failure."

23. Stritmatter, Roger and Lynne Kositsky "The Spanish Maze and the Date of The Tempest", *The Oxfordian, Volume 10,* (2007) pgs. 9-19.

24. Barrell, Charles Wisner. "A Literary Pirate's Attempt To Publish The Winter's Tale in 1594", from T*he Shakespeare Fellowship Quarterly* (April 1946), also available in "The Writings of Charles Wisner Barrell," located on the web at Shakespeare Authorship Sourcebook.

25. Whalen, Richard F. "A Dozen Plays Written After Oxford Died? Not Proven!" *The Oxfordian, Volume 10* (2007), pgs. 75-84.

26. Chamber, E. K. *William Shakespeare, A Study of Facts and Problems, Volume 1*, pg. 253, quoted in Whalen article noted above.

27. Barrell, Charles Wisner. "Shakespeare's 'Fluellen' Identified As A Retainer of the Earl of Oxford" in *The Shakespeare Fellowship Newsletter* (August 1941), available at Internet website Shakespeare Authorship Sourcebook.

28. Brazil, Robert. "Unpacking The Merry Wives" *The Oxfordian, Volume 2.* (1999), pg. 120.

29. Sears, Elizabeth. *Shakespeare and the Tudor Rose.* pgs. 61-63.

30. Ogburn Jr., Charlton. *The Mysterious William Shakespeare*, 1992 edition. pgs. 662-663.

31. Gidley, Fran. "Shakespeare in Composition: The Authorship of Sir Thomas More," *The Oxfordian, Vol. VI.* (2003), pg. 51

32. *Ibid.*, pg. 30

33. *Ibid.*, pg. 31

34. *Ibid.*, pgs. 29-54.

35. *Ibid.*

36. Herberger, Charles F. "Oxford and Rare Manuscript Sources", *The Shakespeare Oxford Newsletter* (Winter 1994).

37. *Encyclopedia Britannica, 1966 edition, Volume 16*, pg. 1167.

38. Ogburn, Jr. Charlton. *The Mysterious William Shakespeare*, pg. 222.

39. Ray, W. J., See his essays "Rollett in Reverse" and "Proving Oxfordian Authorship of 'Sweet Cytherea'" in "The Poetry and Thought of W.J. Ray" online at http://www.wjray.net.

40. Rollett, John. "Secrets of the Dedication to Shakespeare's Sonnets" in Malim, Richard, (General Editor) *Great Oxford, Essays on the Life and Work of Edward de Vere, 17th Earl of Oxford 1550-1604.*

41. The calculation is based on the assumption that Shakespeare could have been either a man or a woman and only needed to look like someone who could have lived near to the author's supposed dates of 1564 to 1616. Therefore the field of candidates for Shakespeare would be limited only to Caucasian people who lived between 1550 and 1650. Therefore I include the total population of Europe and the western part of Russia as my population field. Based on information found on line at the site Tacitus Historical Atlas, I found that the population for all of Europe plus Russia in 1550 was 82.37 million, while the population for the same region in 1650 was 96.2 million. Assuming an average life span of 25 years means that 440 million individuals lived and died in Europe between 1550 and 1650. The stated odds, one in one hundred million, are very conservative.

WILLIAM SHAKSPERE'S SIGNATURES

It is obvious at a glance that these signatures, with the exception of the last two, are not the signatures of the same man. Almost every letter is formed in a different way in each. Literate men in the sixteenth and seventeenth centuries developed personalized signatures much as people do today and it is unthinkable that Shakespeare did not. Which of the signatures reproduced here (next page) is the genuine article is anybody's guess.

— Jane Cox
from "Shakespeare's Will and Signatures"
Shakespeare in the Public Records
British Public Records Office, 1985

Belott-Mountjoy Affadavit, 1612

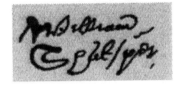

Blackfriars Conveyance, 1613

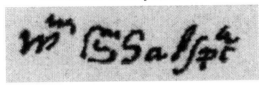

Blackfriars Mortgage, 1613

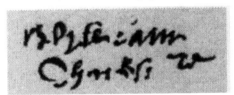

From the will of William Shakspere, March 15, 1616

From the will of William Shakspere

From the final page of the will.
Notice that the first three words are by a different hand
than the last word, 'Shakspere'.

Signatures on this page are from *The Mysterious William Shakespeare: the Myth and the Reality* by Charlton Ogburn, Jr. (1992, pg. 120)

EDWARD DE VERE'S CROWN SIGNATURE

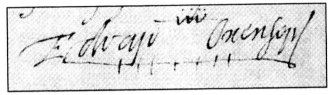

From letter to William Cecil, November 24, 1569

From letter to Robert Cecil, March 22, 1602

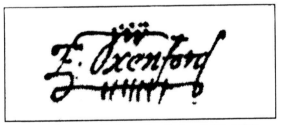

From letter to Robert Cecil, April 25, 1603

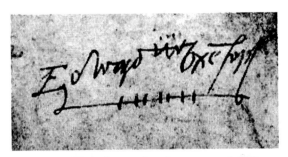

From Hales' annuity document, 1580

LIFTING THE SHADOW

> "An unlifted shadow lies across his memory."
> Alexander Grosart
> writing of Edward de Vere in 1872

Edward de Vere, the 17th Earl of Oxford and a star of the court of Queen Elizabeth I, wrote the Works of William Shakespeare. This has been proven by the investigations of many scholars and researchers who have been working and publishing on the Oxford hypothesis since 1920. For people interested in English literature and history, this is the greatest literary discovery of all time.

Yet many questions remain about Edward de Vere. There are many situations in his life that don't square with the theory that he was a high-ranking member of the nobility who ran into some amazingly bad luck and was ostracized by the ruling class because he wrote plays. Yes, he had some bad luck, but much more prominent in his biography is the good luck that he had, over and over again. Following are some examples.

1. De Vere was raised from about 1554 to November 1558 in the home of Sir Thomas Smith, one of the most brilliant and learned men in England at the time. Smith, who had been a tutor and friend of William Cecil when Cecil was a student, was secretary of state for Edward VI. He was also vice chancellor of Cambridge University and he was a noted scholar of Greek and the law. Because he was a Protestant, he retired from the government during the reign of Queen Mary (1553 to 1558). After the accession of Queen Elizabeth, he was given several posts of great responsibility, including several tours of duty as ambassador to France and, once again, the position of secretary of state from 1572 to 1578. In short, Smith was one of the most powerful and most learned men in the country. How did Edward de Vere, ostensibly the son of a swashbuckling, courageous but unbookish earl, come to be raised in the home of one of the intellectual giants of England?

2. In 1567, Thomas Brinknell, a kitchen assistant of Sir William Cecil, was killed by a wound inflicted at sword point by Edward de Vere. De Vere wasn't convicted of murder. Instead, it was found that Brinknell committed suicide by running onto the end of de Vere's sword. Why was justice so clearly insulted in this case?

3. From 1569 to 1574, de Vere sought repeatedly to serve his country militarily. Except for one instance, when he was sent to Scotland to mop up well after the Scottish insurrection of 1569, his requests were always denied by Elizabeth. Why?

4. From 1569 to 1604, de Vere was nominated to the Order of the Garter sixteen times. In several of these elections, he received only a handful of votes from the dozen or so electors, but on other occasions he received all or nearly all of the votes. Yet Elizabeth always denied his appointment. Why?

5. On September 5, 1571, de Vere's first cousin, Thomas Howard, Fourth Duke of Norfolk, was arrested by the government for his involvement in the Catholic Plot. It had been discovered that he had been planning to wed Mary, Queen of Scots, and to place her on the English throne. Norfolk was placed in prison. In December, 1571, almost at the same moment as his marriage to Anne Cecil, Edward de Vere conspired with others to rescue Norfolk from prison and to provide him with a ship with which he was to flee to Spain. This claim was afterward corroborated twice, in the accusations of his enemies Henry Howard and Charles Arundel, and in the correspondence of the French ambassador. If de Vere were truly guilty of trying to spring Norfolk, why was he never punished?

6. On June 28, 1574, Queen Elizabeth publicly chastised de Vere for some behavior of his which she had found wanting, and de Vere did not receive the chastisement with the proper spirit of abasement. A few days later he fled the country, going with Edward Seymour, the son of the former Lord Protector, to Brussels. He did so without first obtaining permission from the Queen, a criminal act in those days. Three weeks later, on July 27, 1574, he returned to Elizabeth and swore his fealty to her. He was not chastised, neither for his defiance of the Queen, nor for fleeing the country without license. Why?

7. In July 1578 de Vere was one of the courtiers who accompanied Queen Elizabeth on a royal tour, or progress, through the country. During this progress, Elizabeth sent for de Vere twice in one day, requesting that he dance before the French ambassador. De Vere twice declined to do so, saying that he did not want to entertain Frenchmen. Men were killed for less; yet it appears that de Vere did not receive a reprimand. Why?

8. On March 23, 1581, Anne Vavasor, Gentlewoman of the Queen's Bedchamber, gave birth to a son who had been fathered by Edward de Vere. Elizabeth flew into a rage and put mother, son and father in the Tower. De Vere was incarcerated for two months and was banned from court for two years for the offense. Why did Elizabeth punish this offense so severely?

9. In 1586, de Vere was given an annuity of £1000 by Elizabeth. This is quite odd, for two reasons. First, Elizabeth was extremely parsimonious with the royal purse. Secondly, £1000 was an enormous sum in those days. For example, at about this time, the entire budget for state security under Lord Walsingham was £2000 a year. The annuity to de Vere lasted throughout Elizabeth's life and was renewed by James I after his accession. Both monarchs stipulated in their orders that Oxford would neither have to account for what he had done to deserve the annuity nor would he have to explain what he was planning to do with it. Why was Oxford given this generous support from the legendarily parsimonious Elizabeth?

10. On about July 30, 1588, during the critical moment of the break-up and flight of the Spanish Armada off the coast of England, Edward de Vere was assigned the command of the garrison at Harwich, about 40 miles north of the mouth of the Thames on the English Channel. This is where the English military leadership expected that the Spanish were going to attempt to land. De Vere declined this assignment and returned to court. This was dereliction of duty in time of war, surely, at that time, a capital offense. Yet, once again, he wasn't punished. Instead, in November 1588 he paraded in the vanguard of state during the victory celebration and in a popular song of the day he was styled a military hero of the war. Why was his dereliction of duty not punished?

These episodes suggest that Edward de Vere had a special relationship with Queen Elizabeth. This relationship, apparently, lasted all of his adult life and permitted him to act, on some occasions, as if he were a social equal of the Queen. The perquisites of the relationship were only revoked once, after he had had an illegitimate child with another woman and had gone back to live as a dutiful husband with his legitimate wife, Anne Cecil.

One other relic from the life of Edward de Vere throws this possible special relationship into high relief. This was de Vere's signature, a highly stylized, "branded" signature that he used in thirty three letters from November 24, 1569 to April 27, 1603, one day before the date that Queen Elizabeth I was interred and her reign officially was over.

There is a coronet above the name, with four dots above the coronet. Below the name, the initial letter "E", the first letter of Edward, is tied with a long flourish to the closing letter "D", the last letter of Oxford or Oxenford, as he usually signed his name. Exactly and always, seven vertical slashes run through the flourish. Because of the coronet above the name, the signature is called the Crown Signature.

What does it mean? The four dots above the crown signify stars, because the star was a symbol of the Vere family. There are four because de Vere was the Fourth

Baron of Bulbec. The seven slashes in the flourish below signify that he was the seventh of something or other. But of what?

Could the signature be telling us that he was, or could have been, or should have been, Edward VII, king of England? That he was Elizabeth's son?

On the face of it, this is an outlandish suggestion, a suggestion that moves the authorship controversy out of the realm of serious scholarship and into the nut house. But, for the moment, let's consider the benefits of accepting such a theory. It would answer at a stroke nearly all of the enigmas about de Vere noted above. It would explain why de Vere happened to receive such a superb education, why he was not allowed to serve militarily, why he was not prosecuted for the murder of Thomas Brinknell, and why he took to signing his letters with the mysterious Crown Signature. It would explain why he stopped using the Crown Signature directly after Elizabeth was interred and her reign was officially over: he no longer had any chance of becoming king.

It would explain the £1000 "no strings" annuity and why he was forgiven for failing to serve his country during a national crisis. It would explain why he was put in the Tower for fathering a bastard. He was doing more than fornicating, more even than exciting the jealousies of a supremely jealous monarch. He would have been pitching a bastard into the succession.

It would also explain why he was placed with Sir Thomas Smith while he was a young child. On August 2, 1548, Elizabeth's governess, Kat Ashley, wrote a letter to William Cecil requesting that he intervene with Edward Seymour to secure the exchange of an English political prisoner in Scotland. Princess Elizabeth added a postscript to the letter in which she wrote, "I pray you further this poor man's suit. Your friend, Elizabeth." (1)

If by 1548 Elizabeth was already counting on William Cecil as a friend, it is reasonable to suppose that in 1553 or 1554, if Elizabeth was the child's mother and if she was not in a position to see to her child's well-being, she could have asked Cecil for help in placing her son with the best tutor available. It is easy to imagine that Cecil would have recommended his old teacher, the pedagogue and former Secretary of State Sir Thomas Smith. We know that Cecil knew Smith, respected him, trusted him, and we know that the Protestant Smith was out of work beginning in 1553, with the accession of the Catholic Queen Mary. Elizabeth was a brilliant scholar herself. She would have valued Smith's learning and would have wanted the best possible education for her son.

I want to put this bombshell safely off to the side for a moment. Several authors have written books arguing that Edward de Vere was the son of Queen Elizabeth, most notably Paul Streitz in his 2001 book *Oxford: Son of Queen Elizabeth I*. The theory was ridiculed at first but has been slowly gaining adherents. In my opinion, the theory has a lot to recommend it, but, as it is usually articulated, it has some enormous problems. In what follows I want to explore the liabilities of the theory and to offer a theory of my own. So I will ask the reader to accept, for the moment, the hypothesis that Edward de Vere—that is, William Shakespeare—was the unacknowledged, illegitimate son of Queen Elizabeth. The next question is, who was the boy's father?

There are two candidates for the paternity of Edward de Vere. The first is John de Vere, the 16th Earl of Oxford, and the second is Thomas Seymour, Lord Admiral of the English Navy from 1547 to 1549. Let's consider Seymour first.

Thomas Seymour was one of the most villainous figures in all of English history. He was the younger brother of Edward Seymour, who became Lord Protector of the Realm in early 1547, soon after the death of Henry VIII, which occurred on January 28, 1547. As such, while Edward VI was in his minority, Edward Seymour was in charge of the government. After Edward Seymour was named Lord Protector, Thomas began to put into play a multi-tentacled plan to erode his brother's authority and to seize absolute power for himself.

The plan included forging alliances with those nubile females who were either in the succession to the throne, or could be construed to be. Those ladies included Princess Elizabeth Tudor and Lady Jane Grey. In the summer of 1547 when his brother was called north to suppress a rebellion in Scotland, Thomas stayed home and fomented opposition to his brother. About the same time, Thomas Seymour entered into an alliance with a band of pirates who were raising havoc in the English Channel. He allowed them to use the Scilly Islands, his chain of small islands off the coast of Cornwall, as a base. The object was to hurt English trade and to foment dissatisfaction against his brother. Finally, on January 18, 1549, he was discovered in King Edward's quarters while attempting to abduct the king. He was arrested the same day and was executed on March 20, 1549.

Let's go back a few years before his execution to see how he entered into the life of Princess Elizabeth. After the death of Henry VIII, Elizabeth, who was then thirteen, went to live with the dowager Queen Katherine Parr, who had been Henry's sixth and final wife. Katherine Parr was a devout and courageous woman who had done much to establish normal, or at least more normal, relations between Henry and his daughters. Several biographers of Elizabeth have noted that she regarded Parr as the person who was most like a mother to her.

Within weeks of Henry's death, on February 25, 1547, Seymour is alleged to have sent a letter to Elizabeth proposing marriage. He was at that time almost 40 years old. In a gallant and graciously worded letter, Elizabeth (again allegedly) declined his offer. The word allegedly is used advisedly here, because the originals of both letters have been lost and the only record that they were written is that they were published in a book, *Life of Elizabeth*, written by Gregario Leti in 1682. Some scholars believe that Leti may have invented these letters and offer as proof the observation that Seymour's declarations of love for Elizabeth sound very much like other letters allegedly written by other men in some of Leti's other books. According to historian William Seymour, who was a descendent of the Seymours, "A study of other letters published by this author only increases one's suspicion, and no conclusion should be reached on these (letters) alone." (2)

Regardless of whether Seymour had or had not approached Elizabeth by letter, we do know that he moved swiftly to re-establish a liaison with Katherine Parr, through whom he gained access to Elizabeth. The two had courted in 1543, after the death of Parr's second husband, Lord Latimer. At that time, Katherine and Seymour felt a strong attraction for each other, but Henry VIII intervened and claimed Parr as his sixth wife.

But now, with the death of Henry and after a possible initial rejection by Elizabeth, Seymour began to pay court to Katherine. Fatefully, Katherine reciprocated, later telling Thomas in a letter that she had for years fancied him above all the men of England. Thomas apparently began living with Queen Dowager Katherine in March or April of 1547 and they were secretly married in May of that year. Therefore, Elizabeth, Parr and Thomas Seymour lived in the same household from May 1547 until May of 1548.

It is well established that Elizabeth and Seymour had some kind of romantic affair while they lived together. After Elizabeth had left Parr's home, and after Thomas Seymour's more blatantly treasonous acts had become known, Edward Seymour conducted an investigation of Elizabeth's and Seymour's relationship. The investigation revealed that something had gone on between them. Until recently, the historical consensus was that it was a minor flurry of adolescent exploration matched with the unabashed opportunism of a middle-aged scoundrel: some hanky panky may have occurred, but, if it had, it was quickly nipped in the bud by Katherine Parr.

Now, with Streitz's perspective gaining momentum, that view is being revised. What do the documents tell us?

According to Elizabeth's governess, Kat Ashley, Seymour used to go into her room early in the morning while he was bare-legged and she was still in bed. "And if she were up, he would bid her good morrow, and ask how she did, and strike her upon the back or on the buttocks familiarly.... And if she were in bed, he would open the curtains, and bid her good morrow, and make as though to come at her.... And one morning, he strave to have kissed her in her bed.

"He would likewise come in the morning unto her Grace (i.e., Elizabeth) and this examinate lay with her Grace, and there they tickled my Lady in the bed, the Queen and the Lord Admiral.

"Another time at Hanworth, in the garden, he wrated with her, and cut her gown in a hundred pieces, being black cloth, and when she came up, this examinant chid with her, and Her Grace answered, she would not do with all, for the Queen held her, while the Lord Admiral cut it up." (3)

According to Thomas Parry, accountant for Princess Elizabeth's household, Katherine Parr confided to him "that the Admiral loved her (Princess Elizabeth) but too well, and had done so a good while, and that the Queen (Katherine Parr) was jealous of her and him, in so much that one time the Queen, suspecting the often access of the Admiral to the Lady Elizabeth's Grace came suddenly upon them, where they were all alone (he having her in his arms), wherefore the Queen fell out, both with the Lord Admiral and with her Grace also." (4)

Katherine Parr became pregnant in November 1547 and gave birth on August 3, 1548. Remarkably, her ward Elizabeth, with whom she was so close, was sent away to live to the home of Sir Anthony Denny about May 27, 1548. Elizabeth remained living there until October 1548. During that time, Elizabeth was reportedly sick, but the nature of her sickness was never identified, nor was any doctor sent to her.

Katherine Parr died from puerperal fever on September 5, 1548. Elizabeth did not visit Queen Katherine when she was lying in, did not visit her during her final illness and was not present when she died.

The child of Katherine Parr and Thomas Seymour was named Mary Seymour. She was taken care of by several highly placed persons for the first two years of her life. The first of these was Anne Seymour, Duchess of Somerset and wife of Lord Protector Edward Seymour. That arrangement was not agreeable for some reason and the child was moved into the care of Katherine Brandon, Duchess of Suffolk. Early in 1550, after the execution of Thomas Seymour, Parliament determined that the lands that had been previously owned by Thomas Seymour were eligible to be inherited by Mary Seymour when she came of age. Mary Seymour disappeared from history shortly after that. Until Streitz focused his new lens on English history, it had been thought that Mary Seymour must have died about the time of her second birthday. But as we shall see, there may be another interpretation.

Such are the claims for the paternity of William Shakespeare for Thomas Seymour. If we accept that Seymour was the father, we accept that Elizabeth was pregnant when she left the Seymour-Parr household in late May of 1548, and that she gave birth to her child shortly thereafter, in June or July. It would have been her pregnancy and Seymour's passion for her that forced Katherine Parr to eject her from her household. She would have been just fourteen years old when she gave birth.

Let us now consider the claims of John de Vere, 16th Earl of Oxford.

The 16th earl was born about 1518 and became earl of Oxford in 1540. He is something of an enigma, being both a wild man who, according to his first wife, spent too much time with "bad company," and a kindly nobleman who was beloved by all and sundry.

He was very wealthy, his family having amassed property and power since his ancestor, Aubrey Vere, was first awarded several estates by William the Conqueror. His 1562 will lists 78 estates, but author Mark Anderson notes that "he owned some three hundred castles and mansions across England." (5) There are no records indicating that he had gone to a college or university or that he valued learning; rather, there is some evidence that he was a vigorous outdoorsman, a military man and, apparently, a fair and just administrator of his county. He was a kind man whom the local people regarded with affection.

A letter written by Sir Thomas Smith to William Cecil in October 1559 confirms this. "I do assure you I think no man of England, either in Queen Mary's time or any other, could do so much and so readily, with threatenings, imprisonments, and pains, as my lord (of Oxford) doeth here with the love that the gentlemen and the whole country beareth to him. Whether the antiquity of his ancestors or his own gentleness or the dexterities of those that be about thus doeth it or rather all these I think you could not wish it to be better done." (6)

In spite of his high rank, he was not—at least in his early days—involved in court intrigue and he seemed to stay as far away as possible from national politics. However, when called upon to serve his sovereign, he complied. In December 1539, he accompanied his father to Blackheath to receive Anne of Cleves, Henry VIII's fourth wife. In 1544, he was captain of the rear guard under Henry VIII at Boulogne in France. Three years later he sought the restoration of the family's historic office of Lord Great Chamberlain but his petition was denied. Nevertheless, he was allowed to perform some of his office's symbolic functions: he held the king's water bowl at the coronation of Edward VI in 1547. He was one of the twelve chief mourners at the funeral of Henry VIII and also at the funeral, in 1553, of Edward VI. Thereafter, in the crisis following the death of Edward, he declared in favor of Mary Tudor as queen and was commissioned to raise an army in her defense. He did so, and marched toward London in July of 1553. Support for Mary's opponent, Lady Jane Grey, evaporated and Mary was proclaimed queen on July 19, 1553, in London. I don't know if the 16th Earl engaged in any fighting on Mary's behalf.

A story about him will convey some flavor of the man. After Henry's victorious army had secured Boulogne, the Earl of Oxford and the Earl of Surrey had stayed behind in France, and Oxford had been invited on a wild boar hunt. After hunting for some hours, the earl "weary of the toil or else urged by some other necessity" dismounted from his horse.

... "when suddenly down the path in which the Earl walked, came the enraged beast, with his mouth all foamy, his teeth whetted, his bristles up, and all other signs of fury and anger. The gallants of France cry unto the Earl to run aside and save himself; everyone halloed out that he was lost, and none there was that durst bring him succour.

But the Earl ... alters not his pace, nor goes a hair's breadth out of the path; and finding that the boar and he must struggle for passage, draws out his rapier and at the first encounter slew the boar. Which, when the French nobility perceived, they came galloping in unto him and made the wonder of their distracted amazements.... that it was an act made degrees beyond possibility.

But the Earl, seeing their distraction, replied, 'My lords, what have I done of which I have no feeling? Is it the killing of this English pig? Why, every boy in my nation would have performed it. They may be bugbears to the French: to us, they are but servants.' " (7)

John de Vere kept a company of actors which got him into some trouble a week after the death of Henry VIII. While all the town was observing a period of official mourning, John de Vere wanted to have his actors put on a "solemn play" in Southwark, a district on the south bank of the Thames where the Globe theatre later stood. He ran into some resistance from Bishop Gardiner, who petitioned Sir William Paget to keep de Vere's actors from performing. (8)

He was a womanizer, which seems to have gotten him into far more trouble than his theatre company did. He married Dorothy Neville in about 1536; she bore him a daughter, Catherine, in September of 1538. (9) She left him in January 1546 because of "the unkind dealing of the earl," and when the Duke of Norfolk ordered Earl John to reconcile with his wife, the countess declined to go back to him, because of "such a bad company as were about the Earl of Oxford at that time." (10)

Five months after the Countess left him, he married a second woman, Joan Jockey. This marriage was irregular for two reasons. First, it was bigamous, because his first wife was still living when he married Jockey. Secondly, it seems to have been a secret or semi-secret marriage, because few knew about it. This is demonstrated because when his first wife heard a rumor about the second marriage, she had to ask the earl's comptroller, George Tyrrell, if it were true. (11) Also, Jockey lived in a house in Earl's Colne, a small village located about 15 miles from Hedingham, while Earl John continued to live at Hedingham itself. In addition to Jockey, the earl kept a third woman during this period. She was named Anne and was a servant of his tenant at Tilbury Hall, another estate located a few miles from Castle Hedingham. (12)

After his first wife, Dorothy Neville, died in January 1548, Earl John decided to rid himself of his two "outside" women so he could pursue yet another woman, Dorothy Fosser, who had been the governess of his daughter and whom he now wanted to make his third wife.

John de Vere apparently ran afoul of Lord Protector Edward Seymour at just this time. On Feb. 1, 1548, a month after his first wife Dorothy died, the Lord Protector compelled Earl John to sign a contract promising his daughter Catherine, then aged nine, in marriage to Seymour's son, Henry, then seven years old. (13) The bond eliminated the possibility of inheritance by any other children that might in the future be born to the earl; all of the Earl of Oxford's estates and possessions would devolve to his daughter Katherine and through her, to the Seymour family.

This agreement was further enforced by a bond signed on Feb. 26, 1548, which imposed a £6000 penalty on John de Vere should the marriage between his daughter and Seymour's son not occur. (14) In 1550, £6000 was worth approximately $2.4 million in 2009 US dollars.

For some reason, the Earl of Oxford agreed to sign both the initial agreement and the bond. Historians are at a loss to explain what John de Vere did that could have compromised him to the extent that he would sign away his earldom. Alan Nelson says simply that "Lord Protector Somerset (Seymour) extorted an agreement from John" (de Vere). Verily Anderson muses that "Oxford's crimes must have been more than allowing his players to drown the funeral dirge in Southwark, though Surrey had been beheaded for less than that. His proximity by river to the sea and the family's intimate knowledge of the coast could have tempted him to admit unwelcome guests. There are no obvious hints of what his crimes could have been, but certainly great pressure must have been put on a man who had faced a wild boar so calmly with a dancing rapier, in order to make him give way now." (15)

Soon after his first wife had died and these documents were in place, Earl John began to woo Fosser. In this he encountered opposition from Seymour. On June 27, 1548, Oxford's brother-in-law, Thomas Darcy, wrote a letter to William Cecil, who had by this time become Seymour's secretary, telling him of de Vere's continued intentions to wed Fosser. (16) Darcy's letter relates that the two lovers had had banns proclaimed twice in one day and asks Cecil for permission to continue to try to thwart the intended marriage, which was scheduled for August 2.

Then, on August 1, 1548, in a strangely rushed wedding, John de Vere married Margery Golding. The wedding took place, "without royal consent, pre-contract or banns—not at the parish church, but at the Golding residence." (17) A contemporary account states John de Vere had not met Margery Golding prior to the wedding. "And the Duke of Sommerset (Edward Seymour), understanding that the said Earl had good liking unto the same Dorothy, gave order to this Examinant's father that the Earl should not be suffered to have access to the same Dorothy at his house, who took as much care thereunto as he might, and yet nevertheless, the same Earl by his servants, got her to be taken away, thentent (sic; possibly meaning "to the intent") that the said Earl might have married the said Dorothy. But in the mean time before the said Earl met with the said Dorothy, the same Earl in his way toward the place where the same Dorothy was, went to the house of the said Margery Golding's brother, where seeing the same Margie, he grew into such a present liking of her as he presently married her." (18)

Margery was the sister of Thomas Golding, who was an agent of Edward Seymour and who had witnessed the will that formalized the arrangements of the Feb. 26, 1548 bond between John de Vere and Seymour. (19) From her point of view, Margery was only a pawn, but from the Sixteenth Earl's point of view, Margery must have been a kind of booby prize for she must have been under the control of Seymour. Why did John de Vere marry her without having previously met her? Why did he jilt Dorothy Fosser, whom he had been ardently pursuing for six months in the face of opposition from England's most powerful man, in favor of a woman he had not previously met?

Official documents exist that confirm that Edward de Vere was the son of John de Vere and Margery Golding Vere and that he was born on April 12, 1550. There is no birth certificate documenting his birth. However, there is a letter from the king's Privy Council dated April 17, 1550, congratulating the earl on the birth of his son and ordering a gilt baptismal cup to be delivered to him as a gift. (20) His birth date is given at the end of a post mortem inventory taken after the death of the Sixteenth Earl. (21) Percival Golding, Arthur Golding's youngest son, gives April 12, 1550 as Edward de Vere's birthday and states also that he was the "only son of John" in his book about the Veres. (22) John de Vere names Edward de Vere as his son in two wills, those of 1552 and 1562.

Letters also exist from Margery Golding affirming that he was her son. These include a letter to Lord Burghey written in 1563 in which she refers to Edward de Vere as her son. (23) A second letter from Margery Golding exists in which she describes herself, in relation to Edward de Vere, as "his natural mother" and refers to de Vere once as "my son" and once as John de Vere's son. This letter exhibits concern about Edward de Vere's financial well-being and is the kind of letter that a real mother might have written. (24)

After Elizabeth's accession, John de Vere became a more important figure. He was one of the noblemen who accompanied Elizabeth from Hatfield to her coronation in London. Queen Elizabeth resolved a decades-long contention over who exactly was Lord Great Chamberlain of England, confirming him in that position and permitting him to perform the duties of the office at her coronation. He also served as Lord Great Chamberlain at the celebration of the Queen's accession, on January 15, 1559. For the occasion, his wife Margery was made a Lady-in-Waiting to the Queen. In October 1559, the Sixteenth Earl was named part of an official reception party to receive the duke of Finland, who was seeking Elizabeth's hand in marriage for his older brother, the king of Sweden. He rode to Colchester with Sir Thomas Smith and Robert Dudley, the Queen's Master of Horse and, probably, her paramour, to meet the duke. From August 14 to 19, 1561, Queen Elizabeth and her court were guests of John de Vere at his home estate, Castle Hedingham.

The following July, Earl John signed papers arranging a marriage between Edward de Vere and either Mary or Elizabeth Hastings. The marriage agreement makes it clear that neither one was preferred; if one of the sisters died, the other would be the bride; if both were living, then the decision would be by mutual consent. The girls were the sisters of Henry Hastings, the Third Earl of Huntingdon, who was descended from a brother of King Richard III and was thought to be next in line for the throne should Queen Elizabeth die childless. (25) Therefore, John de Vere was arranging a marriage that would link his son with a family that was close to the throne. Assuming that Edward was in fact his son, it was a natural and even a prudent thing for him to do.

A few weeks later, Earl John had written his third will. The will names Edward de Vere as an executor, which indicates that Earl John expected to live at least nine more years, until Edward had reached his (official) majority. The will also names Sir William Cecil and Robert Dudley as co-executors; which was very odd, because there was very little known connection between the Sixteenth Earl and either man. The will was signed July 28, 1562; six days later, John de Vere was dead. Such was the life of John de Vere, the Sixteenth Earl of Oxford.

Now let us try to determine which of the two men was Edward de Vere's father. Accepting that the father was Thomas Seymour would mean that his mother was Queen Elizabeth. As stated above, that would explain the royal favor that de Vere enjoyed throughout his life, a not insignificant benefit in my view.

But attributing de Vere's paternity to Seymour has liabilities. For one thing, Elizabeth seems to have had an equivocal opinion about the man. After his execution, she is quoted as saying, "This day died a man with much wit and very little judgment." (26) That is a remarkably detached comment for a young girl to make about the execution of the man who had deflowered her and fathered her son.

More importantly, part of the evidence for Edward de Vere's identity as William Shakespeare consists of de Vere's glorification of the Vere family in his history plays. He lionized the great hero John de Vere, the 13th Earl of Oxford, but he wrote the less than heroic Robert de Vere completely out of *Richard II*. (See Arguments 20 and 21 in the previous essay.) If de Vere's real father had been Thomas Seymour, why did he identify so strongly with the Vere family? Why is the Seymour family not mentioned in his plays?

An even larger part of the argument in favor of de Vere as Shakespeare relies on de Vere's personal identification with the Vere family and with veracity, the truth, itself. He used the coded signature "ever" throughout his works; he was "evermore in subjection" in *All's Well That Ends Well*;" he wrote that "every word doth almost tell my name" in Sonnet 76; he wrote his first wife, Anne Cecil, a poem in Latin that puns a dozen times on his name Vere, which suggests the Latin word for truth, veritas. How could and why would he have done that if he were not truly a Vere? To have done so would mean that he would have been basing his identity as a great poet, a man who virtually stood for the truth, a man who relied on his identity with the truth to win his way through the most difficult of circumstances, when he knew himself to be not true. I cannot conceive of that as having been the case.

As a final argument against the Seymour paternity I will refer to *Hamlet*, a play which has so many parallels to de Vere's personal life that it is virtually autobiographical. If we accept that the play was autobiographical for de Vere, we accept that every major character in *Hamlet* has an equivalent person in de Vere's life: Polonius was Burghley, Ophelia was Anne Cecil, Claudius was Robert Dudley, Earl of Leicester; Gertrude was Elizabeth, Horatio was his cousin Horatio Vere. In Act III, Scene 3, Hamlet has a conversation with his mother, Queen Gertrude, in which he compares her current husband, King Claudius, with her former husband, King Hamlet. If *Hamlet* has a strong autobiographical component, then, when Hamlet compares the old King Hamlet with King Claudius, what are the inferred parallels? Suggesting to Elizabeth that her former husband was superior to her current one would make sense if he were intending for her to understand that his father, John de Vere, was superior to Dudley. But it would not be a telling comparison if Seymour was his father, for then he would be implying that Thomas Seymour was superior to Dudley. It would be difficult for anyone to argue that Thomas Seymour was superior to anyone.

Therefore it appears that the theory that Elizabeth and Thomas Seymour were the parents of Edward de Vere is wrong. It is an incredibly attractive theory. It is ingenious and wildly sensational. It smacks of passion and intrigue and exactly the kind of ruthless and scandalous behavior that the major players of the era were capable of. But there is something wrong with the theory: it doesn't explain the "veracity," the "Vere-ness," of Edward de Vere. But before we can render a final decision on this question, let's consider a later chapter in Shakespeare's life, his subsequent love affair with Queen Elizabeth.

Venus and Adonis

Letters from the early 1570s confirm that de Vere was first in the Queen's affections during that time. "The Queen's Majesty delighteth more in his personage and his dancing and his valientness than any other," according to Gilbert Talbot, a court observer writing in 1572. (27) The same writer notes that Lady Burghley (i.e. Mildred Cook Cecil, Lord Burghley's wife) was angry at Elizabeth because her attentions were keeping de Vere away from Lady Burghley's daughter, Anne, whom de Vere had married in Dec. 1571. Talbot's letter goes on to say that Lord Burghley "winketh" at all these love matters. Moreover, we know that Edward de Vere sometimes treated Elizabeth familiarly, as if she were a friend who had no particular power over him, and not the Queen of England.

Assuming that de Vere was Elizabeth's son would explain some of his behavior, but there is the definite sense that there were "country matters" involved. As with the filial claim, this carnal one has only a shadowy basis in the historical record. Yet it can be deduced from the literary record left in the plays and in the poems and by combining them with a few telling episodes from de Vere's biography.

Much of the relevant literary record can be found in the play *A Midsummer's Night's Dream*. It is probably Shakespeare's most imaginative comedy and it is the one comedy for which scholars have been unable to find a classical or Renaissance model.

The play centers on three clusters of relationships. First Theseus and Hippolyta, who are to be married; secondly, two couples: Hermia and Lysander, and Helena and Demetrius, whose love is confounded by magic; and thirdly, Oberon and Titania, two fairies whose dispute drives the action of the play.

The dispute centers around a changeling child, an Indian boy who is under the control of Titania but whom Oberon wants. In Act II, Scene 1, Shakespeare writes:

> Oberon:
> I do but beg a little changeling boy
> to be my henchman.
>
> Titania:
> Set your heart at rest.
> The fairyland buys not the child of me.

A second reference to the putative situation occurs a few lines further on in the play. Once again, Oberon is speaking, this time to Puck:

> That very time I saw, but thou couldst not,
> flying between the cold moon and the earth,
> Cupid all armed. A certain aim he took
> at a fair Vestal, throned in the west,
> and loosed his love shaft smartly from his bow
> as it should pierce a hundred thousand hearts.
> But I might see young cupid's fiery shaft
> quenched in the chaste beams of the wat'ry moon,
> and the imperial votress passed on
> in maiden meditation, fancy-free.

These lines suggest that Titania, (which is an Ovidian variation of Diana, which is poetic name for Queen Elizabeth) has a changeling child, sought by Oberon, who is King of the Fairies, which could mean, king of the Veries, or king of the Veres.

A few lines later, Oberon says that Cupid has tried to shoot an arrow at a "fair vestal, throned by the West" (i.e., a virgin who sits on a throne in a western country. England is in western Europe; Elizabeth played the part of a virgin.)

But the arrow missed, or was deflected, or sank powerlessly in the vestal's lunar aura. It was "quenched in the chaste beams of the wat'ry moon" i.e., the attempt to get Elizabeth to love him failed; Oxford's blandishments or charms or charisma were deflected by the power of the Virgin Queen, who dumped the changeling child (but not upon Oxford) and went on being queen, unconcerned about their personal relationship:

> and the imperial votress passed on
> in maiden meditation, fancy-free.

An episode from Edward de Vere's life seems to suggest a crisis of this nature. Elizabeth and de Vere spent a great deal of time together in 1572, '73 and '74. They were together at court almost daily. Elizabeth visited de Vere's estate, Havering On The Bower, on July 19 and 20, 1572. De Vere accompanied her twice when she visited Archbishop of Canterbury Matthew Parker, in January 1573 and on March 2, 1574. Various letters suggest that Elizabeth planned to visit Havering On The Bower again in May 1574 and, when that trip fell through, again in June 1574 and also planned to visit Archbishop Parker that May, in what would have been for her the fifth visit to her archbishop in two years.

According to Oxfordian scholar Hank Whittemore, Elizabeth was virtually incommunicado during April, May and June of 1574. (28) Toward the end of June, she was observed by Francis Talbot, a courtier, as having been "melancholy disposed a good while, which should seem that she is troubled with weighty causes." (29). Then, on June 28,1574, de Vere had a public argument with the Queen.

"The young Earl of Oxford, of that ancient and Very family of the Veres, had a cause or suit that now came before the Queen, which she did not answer so favorably as was expected, checking him, it seems, for his unthriftiness. And hereupon his behavior before her gave her some offense." (30)

A few days later, on July 7, 1574, de Vere bolted for the continent, without the Queen's permission. He was in the company of Edward Seymour, the son of the former Lord Protector of England. We don't know what they were doing, but they may have gone to Belgium with the intention of joining a colony of English Catholic exiles and, perhaps, forming an army of rebellion. The community of Catholic expatriates in Belgium and France were reportedly elated at de Vere's defection.

But, as Shakespeare later wrote, "Conscience does make cowards of us all." De Vere's resolve dwindled and he never made contact with the expatriate community. He stayed on the continent until late July, 1574, when he returned to England, appearing at court on July 27, when he swore fealty to Elizabeth. Edward Seymour died on the continent at the end of 1574.

Keep this episode in mind while we consider a second literary source for the Prince Tudor theory, the sonnets.

For decades, scholars have noted the royal imagery associated with the Fair Youth of the sonnets. Here is G. Wilson Knight, for example, writing in the mid-20th Century.

"The sonnets regularly express love through metaphors from royalty and its derivatives, using such phrases as my sovereign, thy glory, lord of my love, embassy of love, commanded by the motion of thine eyes. At their greatest moment the sonnets are really less love poetry than an almost religious adoration .... The loved one is royal: He is crowned with various gifts of nature and fortune, especially all those beauties whereof now he's king. Like a sovereign, he radiates worth, his eyes lending a double-majesty ... We have clusters of king, gold and sun. Kings and gold come together in the gilded monuments of Princes, and sun and gold, when the Sun's gold complexion is dimmed in the sonnet, Shall I compare thee to a summer's day?, or the young man graces the day and gilds the evening in place of stars.... These impressions are not just decoration.... That the poet of the sonnets was deeply concerned with such themes is clear from the many comparisons of his love to kings and state affairs. His very love is felt as royal and stately. The sonnets are the heart of Shakespeare's royal poetry." (31)

Other, equally powerful, connections illuminating the same phenomenon have been drawn by Leslie Hotson, in *Mr. W.H.* (1964).

It is equally clear that Shakespeare regards the subject of the sonnets as his son.

> As a decrepit father takes delight
> to see his active child do deeds of youth,
> so I, made lame by Fortune's dearest spite,
> take all my comfort from thy worth and truth.
>
> Sonnet 37

> Dear my love, you know,
> you had a father; let your son say so.
>
> Sonnet 13

Indeed, the conundrum that the poet was in love with a youth who appeared both to be royal and to be his son, has given critics monumental headaches for centuries. It was largely this seeming incongruity—especially when authorship was attributed to the actor from Stratford—that led critics to say, with T. S. Eliot, that the sonnets comprised an "autobiography written by a foreign man in a foreign tongue, which can never be translated."

At the same time, a number of critics over the past two centuries have concluded that The Fair Youth of the Sonnets must be Henry Wriothesley, the Third Earl of Southampton. According to Oxfordian researcher Hank Whittemore, the Fair Youth-Southampton connection was first asserted in 1817 by Nathan Drake. Drake's insight was followed by that of an unidentified researcher writing in *The Aethenaeum* (1859). The writer, whose initials were W. C. J., noted that there is a painting from the first half of the 17th Century showing both Henry de Vere, the 18th Earl of Oxford, and Henry Wriothesley, the Third Earl of Southampton, on horseback. Over each of the riders was portrayed their coats of arms with their mottos. The motto of the Earl of Southampton was "Ung par Tout, Tout par Ung," which means, in medieval French, "One For All, All For One."

The researcher goes on to say that there are many examples of that motto being woven into the text of the sonnets and poems of Shakespeare.

He notes that the line

"That one for all, or all for one we gage"

occurs in 21st stanza of *The Rape of Lucrece*.

He notes that Sonnet 8 has the lines,

"Who all in one, one pleasing note do sing,
Whose speechless song, being many seeming one..."

He notes Sonnet 31, which includes the line:

"And thou, all they, hast all the all of me"

and goes on to mention Sonnet 105,

"Since all alike my songs and praises be
To one, of one, still such, and ever so."

The unknown but prescient *Athenaeum* writer concludes, "And in many of the others (of the sonnets) it will be found to be the pervading thought, which I cannot but think brings the noble bearer of the motto and Mr. W.H. into very close union—in fact, they are the same person." (32)

Later the theory was supported by Gerald Massey (1866), Sir Sidney Lee (1898) and John T. Looney (1920), who first identified Edward de Vere as William Shakespeare. After Looney's book, it became easier to connect Southampton with The Fair Youth. But even after Looney, it still took decades to fully understand the significance of the Southampton identification with the Fair Youth.

The second step toward a full unraveling of the riddle was taken by English Oxfordians Percy Allen and B. W. Ward, writing in 1936. In a short article published in that year, Allen and Ward wrote, "Our conclusions were, and are, that Shakespeare, the Dark Lady and the Fair Youth are Lord Oxford, Queen Elizabeth and their son, born to them in early 1575, some months after the Queen's return, with Lord Oxford, from her progress to Bristol in 1574.... Admit that, in May, 1574, Oxford and Elizabeth were lover and mistress, and the whole story of Shakespeare's plays and sonnets, howsoever strange and wonderful—as, indeed, we are told that it is, in the last act of *A Winter's Tale*—becomes a coherent and easily comprehensible sequence of events." (33)

Note that Allen and Ward do not maintain that that child was Southampton. They merely assert that Oxford and Elizabeth had a son.

It remained for Dorothy and Charlton Ogburn to connect all three touchstones —the royalty of the Fair Youth, the sonness of the Fair Youth, and the fact that he was Southampton—in their 1952 book *This Star of England*.

"For the Third Earl of Southampton was the son of Oxford and Elizabeth. He was the 'little changeling boy.' ... It will already have become apparent to the discerning reader that in this story of Edward de Vere, the Seventeenth Earl of Oxford, as author of the dramas and poems published under the pseudonym of "William Shakespeare" we are overwhelmed with a superabundance of material, a weight of evidence. ... Here, especially, (i.e., on the question of the identity and parentage of The Fair Youth) we find ourselves almost confounded by the wealth of testimony; for, not only has Oxford told 'the golden story' in the Sonnets, he has told it in the long and short poems and in the plays, insistently, pointedly, copiously; many contemporary writers have made reference to it; and quite apart from all this, certain external events speak for themselves." (34)

The theory was reintroduced in the great book by their son, Charlton Ogburn, Jr., *The Mysterious William Shakespeare*, in 1992, and was expanded and developed by Hank Whittemore in his 2005 book *The Monument*.

Proof of this theory was noted by early researchers into de Vere, including Percy Allen and Dorothy Ogburn and Charlton Ogburn, Sr. (35). These authors write that on June 24, 1604, Southampton was arrested by government officials and was brought in for questioning. Others who had been involved in the Essex Rising were arrested and questioned as well, and Southampton's papers were seized and read. Southampton was apparently cleared of all suspicion for he was released the next day.

Interestingly, no record of this action exists in the official papers of the English government. However, according to Southampton biographer G. P. V. Akrigg, corroboration of Southampton's arrest was found in the papers of both the French and the Venetian ambassadors. (36) Why would Southampton, who as we know had been released from the Tower just the year before, suddenly be hauled in for questioning on June 24, 1604—*the very day that Edward de Vere died?*

This is proof of Southampton's royalty. It proves that he must have been the son of Elizabeth and simultaneously it proves that de Vere must have been his father, for the arrest occurred on the day that de Vere died.

James must have been aware of the relationship between Southampton, Elizabeth and de Vere. He must have feared that with the death of the father, there was no countervailing force left to restrain the son from trying to seize his rightful throne. This would explain the arrest of Southampton, why it happened on that day, and why no record of it was kept by the government.

Additional proof can be found in the Tower Portrait of Henry Wriothesley, in which Wriothesley is painted as if he were in his cell in the Tower. The proof can be found in the impresa, seemingly a painting that is hanging on the cell wall in the portrait. As with the Ashbourne Portrait considered in the previous essay, the rules governing the use of impresa mean that the details in it speak to the identity or the situation of the subject of the painting.

In the Tower Portrait, the impresa displays a miniaturized cityscape of London. We see the towers of a royal castle in the rear, before which the Tower itself, the royal prison, stands by the Thames River. In the river four swans swim in rough water. Author Elisabeth Sears has analyzed this impresa and has reached a startling conclusion.

"British citizens today still respect the status of these swans as Royal Swans. No one may touch them but the Royal Swan Keepers. In the sixteenth century, tampering with Royal Swans called for the death penalty. The swans in this instance are swimming with some difficulty in very turbulent waters. This could therefore translate to, "Royalty swimming in turbulent waters," and, carrying that over to the sitter being portrayed, he is seen as "Royalty in serious trouble." (37)

So we have multiple strands of evidence proving that Southampton was royal. We have the sonnets, which attribute royalty to the subject of the poems, and we have another line of evidence that demonstrates that Southampton must have been that subject. We have the fact of his arrest and interrogation by the English government, and we have the fact that all evidence within the government for that arrest and interrogation was suppressed. And we have the Tower Portrait, suggesting that Wriothesley was a royal swan swimming in rough waters.

We can confidently say then that Southampton was the son of Queen Elizabeth and Edward de Vere.

Now we can reconsider our original question, who were the parents of Edward de Vere? Remember there are several documents suggesting or stating plainly that de Vere was the son of John de Vere and Margery Golding. At the same time, how can we explain why Edward de Vere enjoyed the special favor of Queen Elizabeth for as long and as steadily as he did? If he was her lover from about 1572 to 1574, that could explain why he wasn't punished for going to Belgium without the Queen's permission in 1574. If he were the father of her son, that would explain why he refused to dance before the French ambassador in 1578. The fact that he was William Shakespeare, and was by 1586 well established in his career as the greatest playwright in the history of the world, could explain why he was given the £1000 annuity. The fact that he was raised with Sir Thomas Smith, and received the benefit of Smith's new theories of pedagogy and his substantial library, could be explained, possibly, by the fact that his father, John de Vere, knew Smith. For the Sixteenth Earl, who was one of the chief mourners for Henry VIII and who performed some of the traditional duties of the Lord Great Chamberlain at the coronation of Edward VI, would have met Smith, who became Secretary of State under Edward.

But would John de Vere have wanted a fine education for his son? We don't know enough about him to be able to tell.

Those points aside, there are still several remarkable instances in the lives of both Edward and John de Vere that are not adequately explained by the supposed parentage of Edward de Vere by the Sixteenth Earl and Margery Golding. Why did John de Vere marry Golding on the day that he met her? And why did he marry *her*, of all people, the sister of one of the men who had witnessed his extortionate and ruinous bond with Edward Seymour? And why did John de Vere die just six days after signing his third will, and just a month after signing a marriage contract between his son and either of the sisters of the Third Earl of Huntingdon? And why did Edward de Vere start using the Crown Signature in November, 1569, a year and a half before anyone had noticed that he had grown to be first in the Queen's affections? And why did he stop using it directly after Elizabeth was buried? Why would Elizabeth have kept him out of the Order of the Garter for his entire life? And why did she not punish his attempted rescue of his cousin, the Fourth Duke of Norfolk? Remember, the Duke of Norfolk was not imprisoned for a minor charge. He wanted to have Queen Elizabeth killed, to put Mary Stuart on the English throne and turn England back into a Catholic country. Attempting to free Norfolk was a capital crime, yet not only was de Vere not punished for promising to provide a ship for his escape, a few weeks later he was rewarded for his near crime by being allowed to marry Anne Cecil. Why? Why was he shielded from prosecution for the murder of Thomas Brinknell? Why was he forced to disguise his authorship of the translation of Ovid's *Metamorphoses*? Why was he subjected to the Shakespearean cover-up, in which his authorship of the Shakespearean works was credited to a front man, William Shakspere of Stratford-upon-Avon?

The evidence is contradictory. On the one hand, records clearly state that John de Vere and Margery Golding were de Vere's parents. On the other hand, facts from de Vere's life suggest both that he was John de Vere's son, and that he had a mysterious, persistent relationship with Elizabeth that both preceded and superceded his romantic relationship with her. So let's go back now and try to determine who his mother was.

There is a great deal of circumstantial evidence suggesting that his mother was Queen Elizabeth. We've already named ten enigmas in his life that suggest he had a long, close relationship with her, a relationship of unconditional love. These enigmas show that he could do almost anything—he could try to rescue his traitorous uncle, he could refuse to dance before Frenchmen, thus humiliating the proud Queen before the French ambassador, he could refuse to accept a military post of great importance during the critical moment of the Spanish Armada's attack on England—with impunity. Then there is the Crown Signature, which suggests that he claimed royalty from 1569—the year, if this theory is correct, that he turned 21—until virtually the moment Queen Elizabeth was buried. There are several additional points from his life and from Shakespeare's work that support this astonishing conclusion.

There is the famous pun near the beginning of *Hamlet*, which takes on a deeper dimension when seen in this light:

> Claudius: How is it the clouds still hang on you?
>
> Hamlet :   Not so, my lord. I am too much i' the sun.
>
> (*Hamlet*, Act I, Scene 2)

There is a passage from *Twelfth Night*, which for centuries has seemed to be merely a gratuitous piece of barbarism, but which takes on a new significance when viewed from this perspective. The passage is found in Act I, Scene 5, when Countess Olivia has chided the clown, Feste, for his tedious humor.

In order to understand this passage, it is necessary to suppose that Olivia represents Queen Elizabeth and that Feste is one of the many personifications of de Vere in *Twelfth Night*. After having been chided by Olivia, Feste replies:

> Thou hast spoke for us, madonna, as if thy eldest son
> should be a fool, whose skull Jove cram with brains for—
> here he comes—one of thy kin has a most weak
> pia mater.

So Feste was Olivia's eldest son. And yet, in the play, Olivia makes no reference to that relationship. She doesn't treat Feste with the deference due to a son and

Feste's sonship has no bearing whatsoever on the plot or outcome or action of the play. So why did Shakespeare write that relationship into *Twelfth Night*? Was it gratuitous or did it point to something deeper?

There is the fact that the 1604 quarto of *Hamlet* bears the royal arms of England on the cover. (38) Under the conventional view of Shakespearean authorship, this is inexplicable, since William Shakspere of Stratford was not an English royal, nor was Hamlet English. The book logically could have had the royal arms of Denmark on its cover, perhaps, but why did it have those of England?

There is the date that Edward de Vere was enrolled at Queen's College at Cambridge University. He matriculated there on November 14, 1558, when he was (officially) eight years old. Queen Mary Tudor died and Princess Elizabeth became queen three days later, on November 17, 1558.

There is the letter written by Arthur Golding in 1563. Golding was at that time employed by William Cecil, Lord Burghley, as a receiver or accountant in charge of administering revenues from the lands of Edward de Vere, who was then a ward of the crown, living under Burghley's management. He also took care of some of the legal business of the Royal Court of Wards.

In 1563, de Vere was sued by his half-sister, Catherine, and her husband, Edward, Third Baron of Windsor. The lawsuit sought to prove that the 1548 marriage of John de Vere and his third wife, Margery Golding, was not valid and that, therefore, since Edward de Vere would then have been illegitimate, the vast holdings of the 17th Earl of Oxford that were being held in trust by the crown under the Master of the Royal Wards, Lord Burghley, during de Vere's minority, would revert to Catherine Baroness Windsor and her husband.

The lawsuit was quashed by Golding's letter. He argued that the Windsor lawsuit offered "grave prejudice of the lady the Queen" and that the case could not legally be tried in an ecclesiastical court, where it had been entered, but only in the Court of Wards and Liveries, which was controlled by Lord Burghley and Elizabeth herself.

Golding's letter asserts that Edward de Vere was fourteen years old on June 28, 1563. If de Vere had truly been born on April 12, 1550, as is generally supposed, he could not have been fourteen on June 28, 1563. It is doubtful that Golding would have made a mistake in such an important matter. (39)

There is the double royalty allusion of Sonnet 78.

> Thine eyes, that taught the dumb on high to sing
> And heavy ignorance aloft to fly,
> Have added feathers to the learned's wing,
> And given grace a double majesty.

Of course, the Fair Youth, whoever he was, had two eyes. But he confers upon grace a double majesty. That means he is twice majestic, hence, twice kingly, hence, twice royal. Therefore, both his mother and his father were royal. We have already demonstrated that Southampton's parents were Elizabeth Tudor and Edward de Vere; therefore, Edward de Vere must have been royal.

Finally, an episode from de Vere's life will again confirm this theory. In the late 1570s and early 1580s, when he was at the height of his prestige at court, Edward de Vere had a love affair with Gentlewoman of the Queen's Bedchamber Anne Vavasor which resulted in the March 23, 1581 birth of their son, Edward Vere. De Vere was thrown into the Tower for two months and was banned from court for two years. In December, 1581, nine months after the birth of his son, de Vere returned to his first wife, Anne Cecil. Two months later, that is, almost a year after the birth of de Vere's and Vavasor's child, Anne Vavasor's uncle, Thomas Knyvet, initiated a series of attacks against de Vere and his retainers. In one of the brawls, de Vere was almost killed. A contemporary letter written by Nicholas Faunt, secretary to Walsingham, states, "There hath been a fray between my lord of Oxford and Mr. Thomas Knyvet of the Privy Council— who are both hurt, but my lord of Oxford more dangerously." (40)

Thomas Knyvet was not only a member of the Queen's Privy Council, but a month before the attacks against de Vere began, he was made Keeper of Westminster Palace.

Elizabeth Sears studies these facts in her book *Shakespeare and the Tudor Rose*. She writes that, because Knyvet was so highly placed before the attack on de Vere, and because he was not disciplined or removed from his positions afterward, the attack on de Vere must have been approved by Elizabeth.

"Surely if he waited a whole year before making his strike, it could not have been inspired by hot anger. It seems, rather, that there was a calculated purpose that drove him to attack Oxford. It must have been done by order of the Queen. Oxford had made too many mistakes, the affair with Anne Vavasor was hard to forgive, but living with Ann Cecil, to whom he had been pseudo-married, made the situation impossible. In order to claim the throne for Southampton, Oxford had to be removed immediately, before he had a family by Ann Cecil. Oxford's moving in with Ann at Christmastime, 1581, only served to bring the situation to a crisis. Elizabeth acted fairly quickly to have him eliminated in as subtle and logical a way as possible," Sears wrote. (41)

Of course, this conclusion only makes sense if Oxford himself were royal. Had he been merely noble, the son of John de Vere and Margery Golding, he could have had as many children as he wanted, and none of them would have been in line for the throne. Therefore, Queen Elizabeth must have been his mother. Now, we have already established that Thomas Seymour could not have been his father and that his father must have been John de Vere. Therefore, the parents of Edward de Vere were Queen Elizabeth and John de Vere.

That was Earl John's mysterious crime of 1547; he had impregnated Princess Elizabeth. That was why he was victimized by Edward Seymour and that is why he agreed to sign away his earldom. The fact that John de Vere wasn't killed for his crime is due to the fact that, in the aftermath of Henry VIII's death, Edward VI was too young and Edward Seymour was too weak to have the popular Sixteenth Earl of Oxford killed. Besides, killing Earl John would have leaked the truth about Elizabeth, ruining her value to the state as an unmarried, virgin princess.

Seymour's secretary, William Cecil, understood this. He persuaded Seymour to allow Earl John to live, convincing him that it would be more politic to force Earl John to sign over his earldom to Seymour than to have him executed. Cecil arranged for the Sixteenth Earl to marry a woman he had not previously met in order to provide a home for his and Elizabeth's son. In doing this, Cecil became Elizabeth's friend, which she confirmed in her postscript written just one day after Earl John's hasty wedding and one day before the birth of Thomas Seymour's and Katherine Parr's daughter, Mary Seymour. And, as Paul Streitz brilliantly deduced, when Katherine Duchess of Suffolk could no longer take care of Mary Seymour, she was placed in John de Vere's household, where she became Mary Vere, Edward de Vere's baby sister, whose birth, like that of de Vere, was not recorded by a birth certificate and who, like her brother, was said to be fourteen years old in Arthur Golding's June 28, 1563 letter. (42)

This theory has much to recommend it. It explains Earl John's otherwise inexplicable wedding and why he was willing to sign over the vast earldom of Oxford, those almost innumerable possessions which had been accumulating in his family since 1066. It explains Elizabeth's lifelong maternal connection to de Vere, and why de Vere simultaneously identified so strongly with the Vere family and with the state of bastardy. He could identify with both because he was both: he was an earl of Oxford and a bastard at the same time.

There is no hard evidence to support this theory. Even the theory that de Vere's father was Thomas Seymour has at least Elizabeth's clandestine romance with the Lord Admiral as evidence, and the fact that they lived under the same roof for a year. But in support of her putative union with the Sixteenth Earl not a scintilla of hard evidence has yet been discovered in the historical record. All that this theory has to support it is circumstantial evidence and logic.

What is worse, the historical record contradicts my theory of the parentage of Edward de Vere. We know that Edward Seymour held an investigation of Elizabeth immediately following the January 18, 1549 arrest of his brother, Thomas Seymour. History tells us that the Lord Protector sent Sir Anthony Denny to Elizabeth's Hatfield residence where he arrested Kat Ashley and Thomas Parry. They were kept in the Tower in harsh winter conditions for two months. We have a letter from Elizabeth to Edward Seymour denying that she was pregnant with the Lord Admiral's child and offering to present herself in person to the Lord Protector "so that I may show myself there as

I am." (43) We have a second letter from Elizabeth pleading with the Lord Protector to release Ashley and we know that he did release her soon after receiving the letter. (44) We also believe we know that while she was shivering in prison, Ashley lamented that she had ever advocated for a marriage between Elizabeth and Thomas Seymour. (45)

This evidence is extremely strong. The letters are beautifully written. They have the ring of truth about them. They are the pathetic cries of a princess fighting for her very life. They attest to Elizabeth's courage, her reliance on God and her absolute insistence on her integrity. Moreover, these letters and other pieces of the historical record apparently come from different sources. Is it possible that all previous historians of the period got it wrong? Is it possible that some mastermind, William Cecil perhaps, put together such a water tight conspiracy that it lasted for 450 years and that, when it began to fall apart, it cast the shadowy ray of suspicion in the wrong direction?

What we have here is a perfectly plausible and deeply moving cover story that obscures and falsifies a recondite, long suppressed but ultimately undeniable fact. Only one version of reality can be true. The historical record must be wrong, or else Edward de Vere's hidden story, what he is telling us in his plays and poems and with his Crown Signature, had no basis in fact. As James Shapiro said in another context, we are faced with a stark choice. We have to choose between the record passed on to us by a cabal of monarchs, politicians and spymasters and the testimony of the greatest poet who ever lived. I'll side with Shakespeare.

Edward de Vere was more than an unlucky nobleman who was ostracized during his life for writing plays. He was actually one of the most tragic figures of all time. Tragic because, in spite of astounding advantages, he had equally astounding liabilities. He was a supreme genius who happened to receive an excellent education from some of the most learned men of his day: Arthur Golding, Sir Thomas Smith and Lawrence Nowell. He had Sir Thomas Smith's excellent library at his disposal in his childhood and William Cecil's even more formidable library at his service from his fourteenth year until his wife's death in 1588. He was born into and lived in the very heart of the English court during its most colorful and most exciting period: the reign of Queen Elizabeth the First, with whom, as we have demonstrated, he was unspeakably intimate.

But, exactly to the extent that he was blessed was he cursed. His vast fortune was sequestered by the crown, he was crushed by debt and fines, at age forty he was destitute; the avenue of martial glory was denied him in his youth and he was led into a profession that was regarded in his day as little better than prostitution or vagabondage. It was an art form that he perfected and transformed; with it he made his country immortal, and yet he knew that his name would never be connected with his works and that the credit for writing the great plays and poems would go to another.

In fact, he was denied his proper recognition and place in society not once, not twice, but six times, and for four centuries. We have already considered the first three, the fact that he was Elizabeth's son and lover and that he was Southampton's father; let's consider the fourth.

Conception Is A Blessing

The fourth great deception that was inflicted upon Edward de Vere involved the paternity of his nominal first daughter, Elizabeth Vere. De Vere himself doubted he was her father. He told Queen Elizabeth, publicly, that he could not be her father, and privately, he told his friend and enemy, Henry Howard, that he could not be the father because he had only lain with his wife one time. His belief that he was not the father caused him to separate from Anne for five years.

One of the most astounding conjectures to come out of the Oxfordian movement is that the real father of Elizabeth Vere was Lord Burghley himself. To my knowledge this assertion has been mentioned in the literature only twice—by James Sherwood in his novel *Shakespeare's Ghost* and by Charlton Ogburn, Jr. in *The Mysterious William Shakespeare*.

The best argument for Lord Burghley's paternity of his own grand-daughter, however, can be found in G.W. Phillips's 1936 book *Lord Burghley In Shakespeare*.

Phillips points out that, in *Hamlet*, King Claudius believes that Ophelia does not love Hamlet. Shakespeare has Claudius say, when Ophelia has gone mad,

> O, this is the poison of deep grief; it springs
> all from her father's death.

That Polonius is indicated becomes clearer when Ophelia sings,

> How should I your true love know
> from another one?
> By his cockle hat and staff
> and his sandal shoon.

These three items are common possessions of religious pilgrims. Lord Burghley often affected to be deeply religious.

When the mad Ophelia talks candidly to the king, Claudius again attributes it to her love for her father, not to her love for Hamlet.

> Claudius: How do you, pretty lady?

> Ophelia: Well, God 'ild you. They say the owl was a baker's daughter. Lord, we know what we are, but know not what we may be. God be at your table.

Claudius: Conceit upon her father.

When Hamlet sends Ophelia his poem, in the long title to the poem he describes Ophelia as "beautified" not "beautiful." Surely "beautified" implies that Ophelia wears a lot of make up and must need basic help in the beauty department, at least in the eyes of Hamlet.

Crucially, Phillips analyzes Ophelia's lines

> Then up he rose, and donn'd his clothes,
> and dupp'd the chamber door;
> "let in the maid"— that out a maid
> never departed more. (46)

Philips does not expressly state the conclusion that Burghley himself impregnated his daughter. But he offers evidence that Shakespeare intended for us to understand that Ophelia loved her father so much that she went mad after his death. I think it is undeniable that Shakespeare also inserted into the text of *Hamlet* weird crackling lightning bolts of dialogue that suggest that Ophelia had a physical passion for Polonius. ("let in the maid, that out a maid/never departed more" and "his cockle hat and staff and his sandals shoon.")

Remembering that *Hamlet* is autobiographical, and that Lord Burghley is Polonius, and that Oxford doubted the paternity of his first born daughter, we are brought to a point of view on the matter that explains why de Vere broke with Anne for five years. Here is how Charlton Ogburn, Jr. explains it. In the first sentence he is referring to notes that Burghley wrote to himself, apparently when he was wracked by doubt over whether the Earl of Oxford would accept or deny paternity of Elizabeth Vere.

> "That Burghley felt the need to write those memoranda is significant. When he felt that need is conclusive to their importance. Both were written long before Oxford had betrayed any misgivings about his wife's pregnancy. Oxford's response to the news that his wife is going to have a child and then that she had had one had been, as we have seen, altogether one of pleasure. I come back to the only basis I can find for Burghley's dreadful apprehensions and his daughter's: Anne had conceived the child after she had last lain with her husband. How could such a thing have come about? Only two possible explanations suggest themselves. One is that Anne's appearance of devotion and loyalty to her marriage and of constancy of nature was deceptive. I strongly incline to the other: that her father was determined as far as humanly possible to ensure the continuation of the marriage and the status of his descendants as Earls of Oxford. Three years had passed since Anne's and Edward's wedding and still there was

no sign of issue, while it had now become impossible any longer to deny his son-in-law a Continental trip from which, given the hazards of travel, he might not return.

Thus, exploiting his daughter's uncommon filial submissiveness and the argument that a child would be the surest means of binding her husband to her, he overcame her compunctions and resistance and brought her to accept service by another male and one of proved fertility.

(Who the other was is beside the point, but I imagine that if the choice had been Burghley's, it was governed by two necessities. First, the absolute minimum number of persons must be in on the arrangements. Secondly, the offspring, since it could not resemble a de Vere, must on no account look like anyone but a Cecil. I leave it to the reader to take it from there.)" (47)

Remember, Charlton Ogburn, Jr. was writing in 1980 or thereabouts, while the world was still of the opinion that Edward de Vere was the Seventeenth Earl of Oxford and nothing more. But now we can confidently claim that Oxford was of royal blood. William Cecil Lord Burghley would have been one of only a dozen people in England who would have known that to be true. That being so, his desire to ensure that the marriage between de Vere and his daughter would continue would have been even stronger than Ogburn could have imagined.

Once again, *Hamlet* gives us a clue to the true relationship between de Vere and Burghley. Hamlet tells Polonius,

> Conception is a blessing, but as your daughter
> may conceive—friend, look to't.

Hamlet, Act II, Scene 2

It is a very odd note, a very ambiguous note. On the one hand, it is as if Hamlet is telling Polonius to look into how his daughter may conceive, that is, to inquire into the dark recesses of his daughter's sexual life. But in another sense, it is almost as if Hamlet/de Vere is telling Polonius/Burghley to look to, that is, attend to, the conception that his daughter will have *in the future*, that is, to copulate with her.

In *King Lear*, the octogenarian protagonist rants and raves against the sea of troubles that has driven him into madness. One of his imprecations alleges that someone is incestuous:

> Tremble, thou wretch,
> that hast within thee undivulged crimes
> unwhipped of justice. Hide thee, thou bloody hand,
> thou perjured, and thou simular of virtue,

that art incestuous. Caitiff, to pieces shake,
that under covert and convenient seeming
has practiced on man's life. Close pent-up guilts,
rive your concealing continents and cry
these dreadful summoner's grace. I am a man
more sinned against than sinning.

— *King Lear*, III, Scene 2, lines 51-59.

It sounds to me that Lear is railing against some external person. It's difficult to identify with certainty who that person is: de Vere certainly knew a lot of rotten people. But remember that John de Vere was murdered by Elizabeth, Cecil and Dudley in 1562. Remember that de Vere was nearly killed by pirates upon his return to England in 1576, and consider that those pirates could have been tipped off by a certain Principal Secretary near and dear to de Vere. Recall, again, that de Vere was nearly murdered by Anne Vavasor's uncle, Thomas Knyvet, in 1582, and consider that, because the series of street brawls between de Vere's men and Knyvet's men occurred a full year after Vavasor had given birth to de Vere's child, the failed hit on de Vere was likely approved by Queen Elizabeth and her principal advisors.

Neither Lord Burghley nor Queen Elizabeth can be ruled out as the intended recipients of this blast from the great poet.

It is impossible to prove either that Lord Burghley was the father of Elizabeth Vere, or that the Earl of Oxford believed that to be the case. We can say, though, that in his two greatest plays he comes right up to the edge of saying so.

A portrait of Elizabeth Vere made while she was a young woman shows a brunette with pinched features, a widow's peak, and a hurt, grasping, unattractive look. If I may be forgiven for writing unfeelingly of an unfortunate lady, she looks like a little weasel. She did not much resemble her proud and beautiful nominal father.

The biography of Edward de Vere suggests that he was both a royal bastard and a royal lover, and that both of these truths were suppressed. His biography also suggests that he could have been the ultimate cuckold, for he was apparently cuckolded by the most powerful and, seemingly, the most virtuous and innocent man in the kingdom, the last man whom anyone, then or now, would be willing to believe capable of such an act: his wife's father.

From the Sublime To The Ridiculous

The fifth instance that Edward de Vere was forced to lie to the world was in the birth of Henry de Vere, whom the world acknowledges, even today, as his son and heir. This relationship, too, is suspect, as we will show.

The best work on this point has been done by Oxfordian researcher John Hamill in his 2005 essay "The Dark Lady and Her Bastard: An Alternative Scenario." My points are a summary of Hamill's work. Hamill contends that, while the mother of Henry de Vere, the 18th Earl of Oxford was Edward de Vere's second wife, Elizabeth Trentham, the father was not Edward de Vere. Hamill argues that the real father was Henry Wriothesley, the Third Earl of Southampton.

Hamill offers several pieces of evidence to support this hypothesis. First, Edward de Vere appears to never have written a poem or sonnet about Henry de Vere. The poems, or most of them, seem to be about Henry Wriothesley; some seem to be addressed to others in his life: at a minimum, Anne Cecil (#117) and Queen Elizabeth (#122). But there does not seem to be any sonnet about a seven to ten year old boy that will redeem the earldom or resurrect the good name of the broken and regretful earl. It seems as if, as far as the poetry is concerned, the 18th Earl of Oxford might as well have never been born. It seems as if Edward de Vere had no feeling of fathership toward Henry de Vere.

Hamill states the Dark Lady sonnets seem to express the thoughts of a man who is married. He writes, "Though he is passionately in love with her, a love that is realistic and mature, he constantly reviles her in angry and insulting poetry. Thus, by his consistent description and his emotional reaction to her, it is clear there was only one Dark Lady. Yet, he never speaks of leaving her; that does not seem to be an option. He seems to be in a bondage that he cannot break. Is he married to her?" (48)

Toward the end of their lives, the 18th Earl of Oxford and the Third Earl of Southampton were comrades in war and politics. About 1620, one of the strongest of English political currents once again involved Spain. The English monarch, King James I, had a son, Prince Charles, and a homosexual lover, George Villiers, the Duke of Buckingham. In order to counter the resurgent power of Spain, James and Buckingham wanted to marry Prince Charles to the Spanish Infanta. For many English people, this was seen as a tergiversation that would nullify the greatest decades of English history, when England had defeated Spain in a twenty years' war. Under the weak leadership of James, it would also lay England open to receiving more influence from the Spanish than England would gain by extending influence over the Spanish.

Southampton, who was in the 1620s a respected elder member of the nobility, opposed the marriage. The 18th Earl supported Southampton, and in June 1621, was arrested for making too bold a speech in support of him. He was imprisoned for several months.

The following year, from April 1622 to December 1623, Henry de Vere was again imprisoned for the same reason. But Southampton reached an accommodation with Buckingham, and the 18th Earl of Oxford was released from prison.

Again, in 1624, both men served as colonels in the Low Countries in the war against Spain. Each was in charge of 1500 English soldiers fighting under Dutch command. They reached a very practical and cordial accommodation with each other to ensure that both social protocols and military expediency were served.

Also, the two men looked remarkably alike. As Hamill has shown in illustrations published in his essay, the 18th Earl of Oxford at age 25 looks an awful lot like the Third Earl of Southampton at the same age.

There is also the evidence supplied by the anonymous poem, *Willobie His Avisa*. Published in 1594, the same year as *The Rape of Lucrece*, *Willobie His Avisa* tells of how an old actor, who is unnamed but whose initials are W.S., advises and abets a young man, whose initials are H.W. and who is referred to as Harry, to bed a married woman named Avisa.

Hamill quotes a 1937 article by Pauline Angell which demonstrates that an element in the design of the frontispiece for the 1594 edition, a crescent moon over the head of an ass (or a stag) (or an ox) meant that the poem was about the 17th Earl of Oxford.

"The crescent was the distinguishing mark of the Oxford crest, which is a boar set apart from all other armorial boars by the fact that a crescent is emblazoned upon it. Crescents are also emblazoned on the stars of the Oxford standard. In fact, these crescents were so thoroughly identified with Oxford that the Queen called him her Turk. And so the horned ass (or stag) embellished with a crescent was as good as a name plate in 1594," writes Angell. (49)

Hamill also notes seven similarities between life situations given to Avisa in the poem and those that Elizabeth Trentham is known to have had.

From all of the above, Hamill concludes that Wriothesley was the father of Henry de Vere, the 18th Earl of Oxford. I agree with his conclusion and as additional evidence point to Sonnets 40, 41 and 42, which suggest that the Fair Youth had bedded the poet's mistress.

Sonnet 42

That thou hast her, it is not all my grief,
and yet it may be said I loved her dearly;
that she has thee is of my wailing chief,
a loss in love that touches me more nearly.
Loving offenders, thus I will excuse ye:
thou dost love her, because thou knowst I love her,
and for my sake even so doth she abuse me
suff'ring my friend for my sake to approve her.
If I lose thee, my loss is my love's gain,
and losing her, my friend hath found that loss,
both find each other, and I lose both twain,

> and both for my sake lay on me this cross.
> But here's the joy: my friend and I are one;
> Sweet Flattery! Then she loves but me alone.

Hamill is not a proponent of the Prince Tudor theory, i.e., he does not believe that Henry Wriothesley was the son of Queen Elizabeth and Edward de Vere. Rather, he subscribes to the view that Wriothesley was the legitimate Third Earl of Southampton and that, as a youth, he was a homosexual theatre-goer and dandy who became the beloved of the older poet. As evidence for this he notes that both the 17th Earl of Oxford and Southampton "were accused of sexual interest in men." (50) He notes that Southampton's second biographer, G.P.V. Akrigg, has gathered evidence indicating possible homosexuality in the young Third Earl of Southampton. "Nothing would be less surprising than to learn the during certain periods of his early life Southampton passed through homosexual phases but, until better evidence is found, only a fool will declare that he did," wrote Akrigg in the mid-1960s. (51)

I believe that Hamill is of the opinion that this eliminates the possibility that Wriothesley was Edward de Vere's son. For Hamill would ask (as indeed anyone would be expected to ask), what man would seek to become the lover of his son?

The same question seems to fuel the most popular version of the Prince Tudor theory. Hank Whittemore, the foremost living proponent of the theory, believes that Southampton was Elizabeth's and de Vere's son and that the passionate and true-ringing love poetry in the sonnets therefore must be symbolic and coded and must have to do with dynastic considerations only. The heart-wrenching grief expressed in the poetry is due to the fact that Southampton was in prison, condemned to die, the stunning apotheosis of the beloved is due to his royalty. To Whittemore, as to Hamill, the idea that de Vere could actually have fallen in love with his son is anathema.

My humble contribution to Oxfordian theory is to point out that the two interpretations of the de Vere-Southampton relationship are not mutually exclusive. Given what we know of de Vere's relationship with Elizabeth; given that de Vere was probably bisexual; given the fact that de Vere had to live with and through falseness his whole life, even while he was pining for authenticity in a false world; given that he apparently recognized no ultimate morality but rather believed that "there is nothing either good or bad but thinking makes it so," and given also that de Vere was a slave to beauty, can we imagine that he could have fallen passionately in love with his beautiful, royal and unacknowledged son—a son who was, in effect, a younger mirror image of himself?

Re-read Sonnet 62 with these illuminations in mind:

> Sin of self-love possesseth all mine eye
> And all my soul and all my every part;

And for this sin there is no remedy,
It is so grounded inward in my heart.
Methinks no face so gracious is as mine,
No shape so true, no truth of such account,
And for myself mine own worth do define
As I all other in all worths surmount.
But when my glass shows me myself indeed,
Beated and chopped with tanned antiquity,
Mine own self-love quite contrary I read;
Self so self-loving were iniquity.
  'Tis thee, myself, that for myself I praise,
  Painting my age with beauty of thy days.

So we see that Shakespeare believed himself so close to Southampton that he regarded them as one person. "'Tis thee, myself…"

Sonnet 20 tells us that they did not consummate this one-sided attraction. Many of the other sonnets tell us that he loved him anyway. Some of the sonnets tell us that he wanted him to be king and that he was in terrible agony when Southampton was condemned to death. Sonnets 40 through 42 tell us that the Fair Youth became, for a time, the lover of the Poet's mistress (or wife). And the lack of any poems about the birth and life of de Vere's nominal legitimate heir, Henry de Vere, tells us that Shakespeare didn't care about him, that he didn't figure in the poet's spiritual life.

Henry de Vere wasn't Shakespeare's son. That de Vere had to live with an unfaithful wife and a bastard son was just another example of the fraud and mendacity that were laid upon him.

Very Like A Whale

Of course, the sixth great scam perpetrated upon Edward de Vere was that he was denied public recognition of his authorship of the Works of William Shakespeare. Now, finally, the reason why the "Shakespeare deception" was perpetrated becomes clear. It was not that the Earl of Oxford was too noble or came from too famous or too respected a family. Indeed, other noblemen had written commendable, popular works, but their names were linked with their works either during their lives or soon after their deaths. One may cite the example of Lord Buckhurst, who wrote *Gorbaduc* (1562), called the first English tragedy, and who was credited with authorship during his life.

Or one could mention Lord Vaux or Henry Howard, Earl of Surrey, poets who were from the nobility and whose poems were published—and whose authorship of those works was acknowledged—soon after their deaths. Assuming that the Earl of Oxford was merely the Earl of Oxford and nothing more, there is no logical reason that Oxford's authorship could not have been acknowledged in 1623, with the publication of the First Folio.

But it was not acknowledged in 1623, or thereafter, and there must have been a reason. The hypothesis here offered supplies an adequate reason. The clandestine and incestuous love affair between The Virgin Queen and her Bastard Son—The Bard—and that other desperate and shameful act of dynastically motivated incest between that Pillar of Probity—Sir Spirit, William Cecil—and his dutiful daughter—Patient Griselda, Anne Cecil—are sufficient reason to explain why the government would not allow Oxford to claim authorship of the Works.

Doing so would have led to scholars to ask the very questions asked here, and, the plotters reasoned, would lead to these very truths coming to light. This could not be done, as Elizabeth and the Cecils understood. They believed that they had formed a great and memorable government. Under their watch, England had gone from a troubled, second-rate kingdom to a first-rate power. Many of their political moves had been brilliant and dexterous, and both Elizabeth and Cecil wanted their names to go down in history, both for the sake of personal glory and reputation, and to light the way so that future governments of the realm could aspire to even greater heights.

Armed with such excuses, they decided that the shameful episodes in the great 44 year reign of Elizabeth should be covered up. Key to this was making certain that the identity of the great national poet, who was both the shame and the glory of the Virgin Queen, would remain hidden. For 355 years, dating from the 1565 publication of the first four books of de Vere's translation of Ovid's *Metamorphoses*, which was given to the world as the work of his uncle, Arthur Golding, until the 1920 publication of *Shakespeare Identified* by J.T. Looney, their deception worked. The name of Edward de Vere would remain obscure, almost a footnote in English literary history, and his greatest works would be given to the world as the work of a second-rate journeyman actor/ entrepreneur, William Shakspere, who had a name remarkably like that of the final pseudonym, William Shake-speare, of the playwright Edward de Vere, who was the 17th Earl of Oxford, the rightful Prince of Wales, (yes, as we now understand, very like a whale), son and lover of Queen Elizabeth the First, and father of Henry Tudor Vere, who should have ascended the throne in March 1603 as King Henry IX of England.

Notes

1. Streitz, Paul. *Oxford: Son of Elizabeth I*, 2001 edition, pg. 75.

2. Seymour, William. *Ordeal by Ambition*, pg. 216.

3. Streitz, op. cit., pg. 77.

4. *Ibid.* pg. 78.

5. For 1562 will see Alan Nelson's papers and documents under Oxdox, at www.socrates.berkeley.edu/ahnelson/. For Anderson's assessment, see Anderson, Mark, *Shakespeare By Another Name*, pg. 2.

6. Anderson, Verily. *The De Veres of Castle Hedingham*, pg. 164.

7. Markham, Gervase. *Honor in his Perfection*, (1624), located in Anderson, Verily, op. cit, pg. 146.

8. Nelson, Alan. *Monstrous Adversary*, pg. 13.

9. *Ibid.*, pg. 14.

10. *Ibid.*, pg. 15.

11. *Ibid.*

12. *Ibid.*

13. *Ibid.*, pg. 16.

14. *Ibid.*

15. Anderson, Verily. op. cit., pg. 150.

16. Nelson, op. cit., pg. 17.

17. *Ibid.*, pg. 18.

18. Streitz, op. cit. pg. 93. This statement was made by Rooke Greene, son of Sir Edward Green, who owned the home where Dorothy Fosser was staying in 1548.

19. Golding, Louis Thorn. *An Elizabethan Puritan*, pg. 231-232.

20. Nelson, op. cit., pg. 20

21. Green, Nina. "The Fall of the House of Oxford," *Brief Chronicles, Vol.1* (2009), endnote 50, pg. 82.

22. Golding, Percival. *The Arms, Honors, Matches and Issues of the Ancient and Illustrious Family of Veer*, discovered in manuscript form in 1940 and noted in Ogburn, Dorothy and Charlton (Senior), *This Star of England*, pg. 1198

23. Ward. Capt. B. M., *The Seventeenth Earl of Oxford*, pg. 22.

24. Green, op. cit, pg. 73.

25. Anderson, Mark. *Shakespeare By Another Name*, pg. 15.

26. Seymour, op. cit., pg. 246.

27. Whittemore, Hank, *The Monument*, pg. 18. From a letter by Gilbert Talbot to his father, the Earl of Shrewsbury, May 11, 1573.

28. *Ibid.,* pg. 21-23.

29. *Ibid.,* pg. 23.

30. *Ibid.,* pg. 23.

31. Knight, G. Wilson. *The Sovereign Flower*, 1958; *The Mutual Flame: on Shakespeare's Sonnets and The Phoenix and the Turtle,* 1962.

32. Whittemore, Hank. *The Monument*, pg. 804.

33. Allen, Percy and Ward, Captain B. M. "An Enquiry Into the Relations Between Lord Oxford as Shakespeare, Queen Elizabeth and the Fair Youth of Shakespeare's Sonnets." in Altrocchi, Paul and Whittemore, Hank, *Shine Forth*, pages 408 and 409. Shine Forth is Volume 3 in their series *Being The Case for Edward de Vere as Shakespeare*.

34. Ogburn, Dorothy and Charlton Sr. *This Star of England*, pgs. 817-818.

35. *Ibid.* pgs. 924 and 1202. The Ogburns note that Percy Allen first understood that the release of the Third Earl of Southampton from his interrogation meant that he had renounced all claims to the throne. However, from their wording, it isn't clear that they are saying that Allen first discovered that he had been arrested and interrogated. That honor may belong to Charlotte Stopes, whose book *The Life of Henry, Third Earl of Southampton* was published in 1922.

36. Akrigg, G.P. V. *Shakespeare and the Earl of Southampton*, pgs. 140-141, including note.

37. Sears, Elisabeth. *Shakespeare and the Tudor Rose*, pgs. 172-176

38. Ogburn, Charlton Jr. *The Mysterious William Shakespeare*, 1992 edition, pg. 757.

39. Nelson, op. cit., pg. 40.

40. Anderson, op. cit., pg. 178.

41. Sears, Elisabeth. *Shakespeare and the Tudor Rose*. pg. 62.

42. Streitz, op. cit., pg. 98.

43. Streitz, op. cit. pg. 80

44. Jenkins, Elizabeth. *Elizabeth the Great,* pg. 33.

45. *Ibid.*, pg. 32

46. Phillips, G.W. *Lord Burghley In Shakespeare*, especially Chapter 4, "Corambis".

47. Ogburn, Charlton Jr., op.cit., pgs. 574 -575.

48. Hamill, John. "The Dark Lady and Her Bastard: An Alternative Scenario", *The Shakespeare Oxford Newsletter, Vol. 41*, (No. 3, Summer 2005).

49. Angell, Pauline K., "Light On The Dark Lady: A Study of Some Elizabethan Libels." in Hamill, John, ibid.

50. Hamill, op.cit.

51. Akrigg, G.P.V. *Shakespeare and the Third Earl of Southampton*, pg. 182.

4

The Secret Life
of England's Greatest Poet

It is a great comfort, to my way of thinking,
that so little is known concerning the poet.
The life of Shakespeare is a fine mystery, and
I tremble every day lest something should
turn up.

Charles Dickens

Born in secrecy in 1548 to Princess Elizabeth Tudor and John de Vere, the 16th
Earl of Oxford, Edward de Vere was raised as the scion of the Vere family, one
of the oldest and wealthiest of English aristocratic families.

In 1562, just weeks after his father had arranged a marriage between his son and
either of the sisters of the Third Earl of Huntingdon, and a mere six days after
having written and signed his third will, John de Vere suddenly died. The son
then became the 17th Earl of Oxford. He was sent to London, where he was
raised and educated by William Cecil, Lord Burghley, who was Queen Elizabeth's Principal Secretary, Master of the Royal Wards and who eventually would
become Lord Treasurer of England. De Vere was therefore raised in the midst of
the English royal court during the fullest flowering of the English Renaissance.

As a teenager he translated Ovid's *Metamorphoses*. It was published in part in
1565 and in full in 1567 as having been translated by his uncle, the otherwise
plodding and unimaginative Arthur Golding. (1) It became the most widely
read and influential book of poetry in 16th Century England. The Twentieth
Century American poet Ezra Pound repeatedly asserted in print that the
"Golding translation" of *The Metamorphoses* was "the most beautiful book
in our language." (2)

In November 1569, when he was 21 years old, de Vere began signing his letters
with the Crown Signature, a stylized signature that indicated he thought he
was the seventh Edward, in other words, that he was in line to become Edward
VII. He used that signature in thirty three letters that we have from him until
April 27, 1603, the day before Queen Elizabeth's body was interred. Thereafter

he used a different signature. This indicates that he understood by no later than November, 1569 that he was a bastard prince of England.

De Vere married Anne Cecil, daughter to William Cecil, in 1571. On his side it was a loveless marriage, and de Vere spent almost no time with Anne for the first ten years of their marriage.

He became the lover of his mother, Queen Elizabeth, about the same time as his wedding to Anne Cecil. A child was secretly born out of this union in June 1574 and was placed in the family of the Second Earl of Southampton, where he was known by the same name as his father, Henry Wriothesley. Upon the death of the Second Earl in 1581, the child became the Third Earl of Southampton. (3) He too was raised as a royal ward in the home of Lord Burghley.

Edward de Vere traveled in Europe between January 1575 and April 1576, making his headquarters in Venice. During his absence his wife gave birth to a daughter, Elizabeth Vere; however de Vere denied paternity of the child and upon his return from the continent broke with his wife and lived apart from her for the next five years. The real father of the child was likely William Cecil himself. (4)

While on tour of the continent, de Vere began to sell his extensive properties in order to finance his travels and to pay his most pressing debts. Sale of his lands increased upon his return to England and de Vere became an important patron of the arts and a legendary spendthrift.

He began writing plays shortly after his return from his continental tour. (5) In April 1581 he was imprisoned in the Tower of London for two months for fathering a royal bastard by Anne Vavasor, a Gentlewoman of the Queen's Bedchamber. This crime of state caused the Queen to banish de Vere from court for two years. The son, who also was named Edward Vere, was raised apart from de Vere; the quality and extent of their relationship remain unknown.

In December 1581, de Vere returned to live with Anne Cecil as her husband. Just three months later, Thomas Knyvet, Anne Vavasor's uncle, began a series of public brawls with de Vere and his men. In one brawl, de Vere was badly injured. This calculated attack on de Vere was performed "in cold blood" and was likely approved by Queen Elizabeth in order to forestall de Vere from having more children and therefore, to prevent there being contenders for the succession. (6)

In June 1583, de Vere was allowed back at court. In 1586, he was awarded a £1000 annuity from Queen Elizabeth, which he continued to receive for the rest of his life. Also in 1586, de Vere changed the crest of his coat of arms, replacing the heraldic boar of the Vere family with a phoenix, which was the personal emblem of Queen Elizabeth and also was the family emblem of the Seymour family. Thomas Seymour (1508-1549), Lord Admiral of the English Navy, is another candidate for the paternity of de Vere. (7)

In June 1588, just days before the attack of the Spanish Armada, Anne Cecil died. Soon thereafter, Lord Burghley and the Queen made arrangements to settle de Vere's longstanding debt. His remaining properties were seized and sold and his three daughters were sent to live with Burghley. De Vere signed the rights to his ancestral seat, Castle Hedingham, over to Burghley and his three daughters. Except for his annuity, Edward de Vere was now destitute.

About 1590, Cecil began to seek a marriage between Henry Wriothesley and Elizabeth Vere. This was to be a dynastic marriage which presumably would have resulted in the acknowledgement of Wriothesley as a prince and heir to the throne and the eventual establishment of a Cecil/Vere/Tudor descendent as a future monarch of England. In support of this marriage, de Vere penned the first seventeen of Shakespeare's sonnets.

However, Wriothesley rejected an alliance with the House of Cecil. De Vere, with decades of twisted family life, changeling children, bastardy and incest modeling his every move, apparently fell in love with Southampton himself. This is the most obvious interpretation of the sonnets; other interpretations maintain that the sonnets are written in poetic code and that when the poet is urging the Fair Youth to marry or is proclaiming his many virtues, he is really saying that he should continue the House of Tudor and the royal blood of Southampton should be acknowledged by the failing Elizabeth. Both interpretations may be correct; understanding the sonnets in the light of de Vere's biography remains one of the most difficult problems in English literature. (8)

Edward de Vere married Elizabeth Trentham in 1591. Trentham promptly had an affair with Southampton; this union resulted in the 1593 birth of Henry de Vere, who was presented to the world fraudulently as de Vere's son and heir. Edward de Vere seems never to have written a line of poetry about Henry de Vere, but the 18th Earl of Oxford and the Third Earl of Southampton remained comrades in war and in politics throughout their lives. (9)

About 1592 de Vere secured the services of an uneducated actor and theatrical entrepreneur from Stratford upon Avon, William Shaksper or Shakspere, to act as his front man. Shakspere was given a sinecure and small supporting roles with the Lord Chamberlain's Men. Thereafter, de Vere began to revise his plays and to publish them, at first anonymously and, after the 1598 death of William Cecil, under the pseudonym of William Shakespeare (or Shake-speare.) He continued to write new plays throughout the 1590s and early 1600s.

In 1596, Southampton offered to assist the aging Queen Elizabeth in mounting a horse. Elizabeth flew into a rage and Southampton's star began to sink from that episode. Southampton aligned himself with another of Elizabeth's favorites, Robert Devereaux, the Second Earl of Essex, eventually marrying his niece, Elizabeth Vernon. In defiance of Queen Elizabeth's orders, Southampton accompanied Essex on various military campaigns. When Essex's ill-fated mismanagement of the Irish War (1599) resulted in catastrophe and disgrace, Southampton stood by Essex. When Essex attempted, by dint of the Essex Rising (February 8, 1601) to break out of the political stranglehold that had been constructed for him by Elizabeth's secretary (and William Cecil's son) Robert Cecil, he and Southampton were captured and imprisoned. Edward de Vere sat on the jury of peers that sentenced both men to death.

Essex was executed on February 25, 1601. Southampton's death sentence was commuted to life in prison and he remained confined in the Tower for the next two years. Much of the sorrow and anguish of Shakespeare's sonnets can be attributed to the hopelessness and seeming injustice of Southampton's situation.

Queen Elizabeth died on March 24, 1603. Southampton was released from prison on April 10, 1603, a result of nearly the first order to come from King James I. Sonnet 107 is Shakespeare's reflection on that happy moment. Edward de Vere died on June 24, 1604. William Shakspere left London in that year and spent the rest of his life in obscure and litigious retirement in Stratford upon Avon. In the fall and winter of 1604-1605, King James hosted the world's first Shakespeare festival, during which eight Shakespeare plays were performed over a 16 week period. (10) The flawed bad quarto of *Hamlet* was published in 1603; the corrected good quarto of *Hamlet*, with the emblem of the English royal arms on the cover, was published in 1604. (11)

The First Folio, containing 36 plays of Shakespeare, was published in 1623. It was edited by Ben Jonson, who was a retainer of the Earl of Pembroke, and was likely funded by the two "incomparable brethren," the earls of Pembroke and Montgomery, who were de Vere's son-in-law (Montgomery) and that earl's brother (Pembroke). Because of de Vere's explosive relationship to Elizabeth and Southampton (who was then still alive), it was decided to maintain the ruse that the author of the plays was an uneducated genius from the provinces, and one who, moreover, could scarcely write his name.

The 37th Shakespearean play, *Pericles*, which explores the themes of incest and prostitution, was eventually acknowledged as a work of William Shakespeare and was incorporated into the second edition of the Third Folio in 1664.

As the Stratfordian model of the Shakespeare's biography breaks down, the Shakespearean canon may be expanded. At a minimum, *The Famous Victories of Henry the Fifth*, *Thomas of Woodstock*, *Edmund Ironside* and *Sir Thomas More* should now be considered Shakespeare's. As scholarship continues to scrape away the encrustations of centuries of error, perhaps more titles will be added to that body of desire, the plays and poems of William Shakespeare.

NOTES

1. It is highly unlikely that the Puritan Golding would have been inclined to translate Ovid. Other scholarship has revealed that for the first ten years of Golding's career, he translated one work at a time, except for the period that he was working on *The Metamorphoses*, when he was translating two works at a time. See Altrocchi, Paul, "Edward de Vere as Translator of Ovid's *Metamorphoses*," *The Shakespeare Oxford Society Newsletter*, Spring 2005, and Saunders, Sam, "Arthur Golding's First Decade of Translation: a Brief Examination," *The Shakespeare Oxford Society Newsletter*, Summer 2005.

2. Pound praised the Golding translation in print as "the most beautiful book in our language" or "the most beautiful book in the language" three times. Ovid, *Ovid's Metamorphoses*, edited by Jonathan Frederick Nims, (2000), pg. xiii.

3. Whittemore, Hank. *The Monument* and Sears, Elisabeth, *Shakespeare and the Tudor Rose*.

4. Phillips, G.W. *Lord Burghley and Shakespeare*. Dynastic considerations prompted Lord Burghley to impregnate his daughter in order to forestall a pending divorce between Anne Cecil and de Vere. This dark secret is hinted at in Ophelia's mad speeches in Hamlet. See also Charton Ogburn, Jr. *The Mysterious William Shakespeare*, 1992 edition, pgs. 574-575.

5. Clarke, Eva Turner. *Hidden Allusions in Shakespeare's Plays*.

6. Sears, Elisabeth. *Shakespeare and the Tudor Rose*, pgs 61-63.

7. For information on the coat of arm change, Burris, Barbara. "Oxford's New Coat of Arms in 1586," *Shakespeare Matters*, Summer, 2003. For a detailed account of putative connection between Princess Elizabeth and Thomas Seymour, see Streitz, Paul, *Oxford: Son of Queen Elizabeth I*.

8. Whittemore, Hank. *The Monument*. It contains a brilliant exposition of this other interpretation.

9. Hamill, John. "The Dark Lady and Her Bastard: An Alternative Scenario," *The Shakespeare Oxford Society Newsletter*, Summer 2005. This scenario would explain Sonnets 40, 41 and 42, in which the poet complains that the poet's mistress (perhaps but not necessarily the Dark Lady) has seduced the Fair Youth.

10. Malim, Richard. "The Spanish Maze," in Malim, Richard (editor), *Great Oxford: Essays on the Life and Work of Edward de Vere, Seventeenth Earl of Oxford, 1550-1604*, pg. 284. Malim theorizes that the otherwise lost play titled *The Spanish Maze* was *The Tempest*, performed under an alternate title.

11. Ogburn, Charlton, Jr. *The Mysterious William Shakespeare*, pg. 757.

RECOMMENDED READING

This information was compiled by
Willits, California scholar WJ Ray and the author.

Shakespeare Identified by J.T. Looney (1920)

This seminal work in Oxfordian theory provides a brief overview of what is wrong with the Stratfordian hypothesis. It recounts how Looney deduced that Edward de Vere was Shakespeare and provides strong evidence taken from de Vere's published poetry and his biography that he wrote the works of Shakespeare. John Galsworthy called this book, "The greatest detective story I have ever read."

The paperback facsimile version of the original 1920 edition is available from Concordia University Bookstore for $22 plus $2.25 shipping. Another edition of *Shakespeare Identified* is from Minos Publishing Company and costs $150 for a two volume hardbound set. Volume I is Looney's work plus de Vere's poems. Volume II, entitled *Oxfordian Vistas*, is a collection of essays in the field of Oxfordian studies written between 1930 and 1975. Both volumes come with dozens of illustrations and colored prints of classic paintings. Any collector or serious student will appreciate this edition.

Website is at ruthmiller.com

Hidden Allusions in Shakespeare's Plays by Eva Turner Clark (1931)

This fascinating study reorders the composition of Shakespeare's plays, based on evidence that they were written by Edward de Vere, the 17th Earl of Oxford. The author bases her conclusions on de Vere's biography and on references to historical events found in the plays. The result is a chronology of plays that makes more sense than the conventional Stratfordian sequence. She posits that the entire collection of plays was written twelve years earlier than traditionally supposed.

Available for $75 from Concordia University bookstore or from Minos Publishing Company for the same price.

This Star of England by Dorothy and Charlton Ogburn, Sr. (1952, 1296 pps.)

This tome focuses on the life of Oxford—how the life illuminates the text of Shakespeare, and how the text illuminates the life of Oxford. It initiated the second generation of Oxfordian investigations.

Out of print but available from used book stores via the Internet.

The Mysterious William Shakespeare: The Myth and the Reality by Charlton Ogburn, Jr. (1984, 1992)

Magisterial work in two sections. The first section demolishes the Stratfordian hypothesis; the second part traces the life of Oxford and shows how innumerable details in Oxford's life show up in the plays. The author is probably the best writer of all Oxfordians. He begins the third generation of Oxfordian lore.

Essential reading. Available from Concordia books, $40.00.

Shakespeare Revealed in Oxford's Letters by William Plumer Fowler (1986).

Have you ever wanted to hold a letter from William Shakespeare in your hand? Now you can, forty-four of them, each exhaustively scrutinized by Fowler to demonstrate linguistic parallels between de Vere's letters and the plays and poems of William Shakespeare. Astounding, but slow going.

Available from Concordia University Bookstore and Minos Publishing Company.

The Seventeenth Earl of Oxford, 1550 to 1604 by B. M. Ward (1928)

This is the first full-length biography of the Earl of Oxford, written three centuries after his death and eight years after the publication of Looney's book. Sticks to the facts, without emphasizing how the life affected the works. In fact, the author does not fully espouse (at least, not in this book) the view that de Vere wrote the works of Shakespeare. His focus is on excavating the life from the ruins of time.

Available as a spiral bound, photocopy reprint from Concordia University Bookstore and from Minos Publishing Company.

Chasing Shakespeares by Sarah Smith. (2004)

A work of fiction. Two American Shakespeare scholars journey to England to research a doctoral thesis, during which visit they stumble on literary evidence that it was Edward de Vere, the 17th Earl of Oxford, who must be the author of the Shakespeare canon. The author deftly and delightfully weaves in facts about Oxford together with a growing sense of wonder and intellectual adventure. A very enjoyable read.

Available from Concordia University bookstore or from on-line booksellers such as Amazon.com.

Shakespeare By Another Name by Mark Anderson (2005)

Another fine biography, this one incorporates discoveries unearthed during the period from roughly 1990 to 2004. The argument in favor of de Vere as the author has by this time become quite detailed and convincing, and Anderson is a good representative of contemporary Oxfordian thought. Available through on-line book purveyors such as Amazon.com or through the author at www. Shakespearebyanothername.com

The Monument by Hank Whittemore (2005)

This work expounds the Prince Tudor hypothesis, i.e., that the sonnets tell the story, in symbolic and sometimes coded language, of Oxford's emotional and spiritual agony because of the succession controversy before the death of Elizabeth I. Henry Wriothesley, Third Earl of Southampton is posited as having been Oxford's son by Queen Elizabeth. He was sentenced to life in prison for his part in the Essex Rebellion of 1601. Just as William Plumer Fowler did with the letters, Whittemore dissects each line and phrase of the sonnets in order to expound their true meaning. In a controversial work, Whittemore may finally, after 400 years, have solved the riddle of the sonnets. However, it must be said that this book is best suited for serious scholars.

Order through book stores (from Baker & Taylor distributors), from Concordia University Bookstore, or at Amazon.com

The Monument: An Abridged Introduction by Hank Whittemore

Privately printed by the author, this slim volume is an introduction to the problems posed by the sonnets and is designed for the high school and college student. It proposes that the answer to the riddle is that the story told by the sonnets is allegorical: the crucial event of the sonnets was the imprisonment of Henry Wriothesley, Third Earl of Southampton for his part in the Essex Rebellion of February 8, 1601. The author reviews his theory that the 154-sonnet sequence is a tightly structured 'monument' to the lawful King Henry IX, with a twenty-six poem introduction, a 100 poem center, a twenty-six poem denouement and a two poem coda. This volume does not include Whittemore's line by line exegesis of each poem as does his 918 page study, *The Monument*, noted above.

The Abridged Introduction is available for $10 (includes shipping) from the author, Hank Whittemore, PO Box 549, Nyack NY 10960.

The Secret Love Story In Shakespeare's Sonnets by Helen Heightsman Gordon, (Xlibris 2008)

This trim volume looks at the sonnets through a different perspective from *The Monument*. While recognizing that Edward de Vere is the author, Gordon interprets the the sonnets as the ordered compilation by the mature poet over a lengthy period. Some of the poems are addressed to de Vere's mistress Anne Vavasour, some are to his wives, Anne Cecil and Elizabeth Trentham, and some to the great love of his life, Elizabeth Tudor, Queen of England. Gordon is much less emphatic than Whittemore on how the sonnets reflect de Vere's relationship with Henry Wriothesley, Third Earl of Southampton. It is a fine study, at times brilliant, and opens doors into understanding those baffling sonnets.

Hardcopies available from the author, Helen Heightsman Gordon, PO Box 6724, Santa Barbara, California, 93160 —$27 plus $3 shipping ($5 priority mail), or from the publisher, Xlibris, ISBN 978-1-4134-9375-7. Paperback available from Xlibris [www.xlibris.com/bookstore] or from online bookstores.

Shakespeare's Unorthodox Biography by Diana Price (2001)

A magnificent demolition of scholarly and literary arguments which support the Stratfordian hypothesis. Written without rancor, it is probably (along with *The Mysterious William Shakespeare*) the best book to offer to Stratfordians. Although Price does not advocate for de Vere as the author, she concludes that the man from Stratford cannot be the author.

This book is available from Concordia University Bookstore.

Edward de Vere's Geneva Bible by Roger Stritmatter (2001)

Stritmatter was the first doctoral candidate to successfully enter an Oxfordian thesis in the United States. His work focuses on interpreting the marginalia and underlinings found in de Vere's copy of the Geneva Bible. This copy is on display at the Folger Shakespeare Library in Washington, D.C. In it, Stritmatter found about a thousand verse-markings and notes in de Vere's handwriting. One-fifth of the noted verse-subjects reappeared in the works of Shakespeare, filtered through de Vere's idiomatic style but unmistakable as specific Biblical references and homilies. Stritmatter examined several of the parallels in thorough scholarly detail.

Available from Concordia Books, $60 plus $6 for shipping.

Players by Bertram Field.

An overview of the authorship question, written for the general reader. The author looks carefully at the possibility that the Stratford man wrote the works of Shakespeare and concludes that it is doubtful that he did so. He then examines the candidacy of several possible authors, including Christopher Marlowe, Queen Elizabeth, Francis Bacon, Edward de Vere and others. He makes no final determination, but fantasizes that it could have been de Vere, working with the help of stage veteran Shakspere, who helped to "dumb down" the plays to make them palatable for the general public. A fun read and a good, non-partisan overview of the authorship question.

Available from Concordia University Bookstore for $30.

Great Oxford edited By Richard Malim

A collection of thirty-nine essays from the archives of the De Vere Society of England. The essays examine various aspects of the intersection of the life of de Vere and the works of Shakespeare, for example, the impact of de Vere's presumed visit to the studio of Titian in Venice in 1575, and how that visit affected de Vere's conception of Adonis in *Venus and Adonis*. The essays are excellent and serve to convince, beyond a doubt, that Edward de Vere is the author.

Available from Concordia University Bookstore.

Shakespeare and the Tudor Rose by Elisabeth Sears. (2002, 218 pages.)

Elisabeth Sears has written a history of the secret relationship between Queen Elizabeth, Edward de Vere and their son, Henry Wriothesley, the Third Earl of Southampton. Since this astounding saga has long been a state secret, any records that might provide official proof of the relationship have long been suppressed. Nevertheless, using available historical and literary sources, keen logic and considerable powers of intuition, Sears illuminates both Edward de Vere's life and the context and meaning of his literary work as William Shakespeare. Highly recommended.

Available from Meadow Geese press, Box 345, Marshfield Hills, Massachusetts 02051 for $22 plus shipping.

Alias Shakespeare by Joseph Sobran (1997, 300 pages.)

An excellent introduction to the life of the Earl of Oxford and to the authorship controversy. It offers biographies of both the earl and the Stratford man and a survey of the problems and leaps of faith involved when attributing the works of Shakespeare to William Shakspere of Stratford.

Probably more than any other major Oxfordian book, *Alias Shakespeare* is characterized by its calm, reasonable approach and its tone of respect toward the Stratfordian camp. (Sobran confesses to having formerly been a Stratfordian.) For that reason *Alias Shakespeare* is probably (next to *Shakespeare Identified* by J.T. Looney) the best book to offer to the uninitiated or to those minds have expressed the slightest aptitude for opening on the subject of the authorship question.

The appendices are excellent, especially Appendix 2, which demonstrates how individual phrases from Oxford's published poetry are repeated or echoed in the writings of William Shakespeare.

The book is out of print but is available from online used and rare book sources.

Oxford: Son of Elizabeth I by Paul Streitz. (2001, 317 pages)

Oxford: Son of Elizabeth I hypothesizes that the documented romance in 1548 between Princess Elizabeth Tudor and her step-father, Lord Admiral Thomas Seymour, went well beyond kissing and hugging and that, as a result, Elizabeth at age 14 bore a son, who was raised as Edward de Vere, who was Shakespeare.

The author offers considerable scholarship to show that it could have happened and considerable exegesis to argue that it did happen. As I write (Sept. 2010) Streitz's theory is moving toward acceptance on the part of several major Oxfordian writers.

Available from Oxford Institute Press, 8 William Street, Darien, Connecticut. 06820 for $14.50.

Shakespeare's Lost Kingdom by Charles Beauclerk. (2010, 430 pages.)

Literary criticism of Shakespeare's works based on the idea that he was Elizabeth's son and lover. The murky conjectures and niggling nescience of orthodox Shakespearean criticism evaporate under the lens of this most current and most complete understanding of de Vere's life to yield the most riveting and illuminating Shakespearean criticism I have ever read.

This is a new book published by Grove Press.

SOURCES FOR BOOKS

Concordia University Bookstore, 6400 N.E. 29th Avenue, Portland Oregon 97211 Order desk: (503) 280-8502

Minos Publishing Company, P.O Box 1309, Jennings, Louisiana 70546 http://www.ruthmiller.com

OTHER SOURCES OF INFORMATION ABOUT DE VERE

The Shakespeare Oxford Society

Founded in 1957, this is the oldest Oxfordian group in America. A $50 annual membership supports ongoing outreach and promotional work, and includes four newsletters and *The Oxfordian*, their annual literary journal.

To join, write The Shakespeare Oxford Society, PO Box 808, Yorktown Heights, NY 10598 or phone at (914) 962-1717. Subscriptions can be paid online at shakespeare-oxford.com

The Shakespeare Fellowship

Founded in 2001, this is a bit more lively and iconoclastic group than the Shakespeare Oxford Society. The purpose of the Shakespeare Fellowship is to promote public awareness and acceptance of the authorship of the Shakespeare Canon by Edward de Vere.

To join, write them at P.O. Box 421, Hudson, MA 01749 or contact them online at shakespearefellowship.org/

The De Vere Society

An advocacy group for Edward de Vere, based in England. To join, go to the organization's website at www.deveresociety.co.uk

Shakespeare Identified by Michael A'Dair and WJ Ray (2006)

Authors WJ Ray and Mike A'Dair gave a lecture under this title in their hometown of Willits, California in April 2006, on the Oxfordian hypothesis. The lecture covers such topics as: Why Shakspere Can't Be Shakespeare and the Life of Edward de Vere, and offers a look at the plays and sonnets with fresh eyes.

50 page, spiral-bound booklet available for $23 (includes shipping).
Pay on line with PayPal or credit-card
http://wjray.net/shakespeare_papers/sales.htm
or mail to: The Verius Project, 22641 East Side Road, Willits, California 95490.

DVD of *Shakespeare Identified* is available from Andrew Wright.
Cost: $20, plus $3 shipping and handling.
E-mail: andrew_wright@earthlink.net.

The Poetry and Thought of WJ Ray

Several incisive essays by WJ Ray, many of them on the Oxford hypothesis. Available online at wjray.net

About the Author

Mike A'Dair was born in Oakland, California in 1951 and was raised just down the Nimitz Freeway in San Leandro. He attended California State University at Hayward for two years before leaving in 1971. Thereafter he lived in San Francisco and in Berkeley.

Since 1981, he has lived in Willits, a small town on the Golden State's north coast. A married man, he is an organic gardener and cares for a small flock of chickens.

A'Dair is the author of a book of poems, *Funerary Gleams*, and two plays, *American Peace* and *The Growers*.